A BLACK COUNTR PUBLICATI

First Impression: September 1968
Second Impression: March 1969
Third Impression July 1970
Fourth Impression: June 1972
Fifth Impression: November 1974
Sixth Impression: February 1977
Seventh Impression: May 1979
Eighth Impression: March 1992
Ninth Impression: August 1997
Tenth Impression: February 2001
Eleventh Impression: October 2005
Twelfth Impression; September 2015

Over 49,000 copies sold

Cover Design by Shirley Bonas

C O N T E N T S

Classification is flexible and intended only as a general guide. Many stories under one heading would be equally suited to another.

The collection of
stories in this
volume is based on
the original Black
Country Stories
published by T. H.
Gough, with many
'new' ones added.

The stories were
revised and edited
by the late Harold
Parsons, former editor
of The Blackcountryman.

Publication is by
The Black Country
Society, by arrangement
with the Executors
of Mr. Gough's estate.

The Black Country Society

The term 'The Black Country' was coined in the mid-19th Century to describe that area of the South Staffordshire coalfield where the 'thick coal' lay.

Over a 150 square mile area some 100 small industrial communities developed, and by the late 1890s a couple of dozen of them were of sufficient size, perhaps when linked with some of their neighbours, to have their own local councils. Since that time there have been several local government reorganisations and after that of 1974 all of the townships of the Black Country were absorbed into the four Black Country Metropolitan Boroughs of Dudley, Sandwell, Walsall and Wolverhampton. In December 2000 Wolverhampton was granted city status.

The Black Country Society was founded in 1967 by enthusiasts, led by Dr John Fletcher, who felt that the Black Country did not receive its fair share of recognition for its great contribution to the industrial development of Britain and the world.

The Society grew out of the Dudley Canal Trust Preservation Society, which had successfully campaigned to save Dudley Canal Tunnel, threatened with closure by the British Waterways Board and British Rail. The preserved tunnel linking the Birmingham Canal System and the canals of the Stour Valley, with links to the River Severn, is now a major attraction at the Black Country Living Museum.

The stated aim of the Society is to *"foster interest in the past, present and future of the Black Country"*. Its voice calling for the establishment of a local industrial museum at a meeting on 6 October 1968 was one of the first on the subject.

The Society has been a major publisher of material on the Black Country, and still produces books and digital productions into the 21st century. Many of our early works are regularly reprinted, including this one. Our major publication is the quarterly magazine, *The Blackcountryman*, which has 96 pages of articles, information and news on Black Country matters and events. For more details please visit our website:

www.blackcountrysociety.co.uk

editor@blackcountrysociety.co.uk

Introduction by the late Billy Russell

SOME forty or so years ago I told a story from the stage of a theatre in Glasgow. Laugh . . . I thought they would never start. And they didn't! The story was about a character from the Black Country. I thought it was a funny story. My audience showed in their silence that it had fallen on stony ground. There is, I have learned through many miles of travel, a definite geography of humour. What makes folk laugh in say, Newcastle-upon-Tyne, would not raise a titter outside a radius of seventy-five miles. Real 'scouse' Liverpool humour has an even more restricted appeal. Regional humour is only really appreciated to the full if one is acquainted with the locality, characters, customs and living and working conditions of the people.

This book of Black Country Stories will, I know, raise many a laugh from the natives and those who have lived in the region long enough to get the atmosphere, know the people, and gain some knowledge of the multifarious industries carried on in the district. A great deal of the humour is evolved from some native utterance which has struck the listener as comical, and the original unintentionally 'comic' saying has been trimmed, doctored and re-phrased to make a good joke with a punch.

5

In the First World War I served in the South Staffordshire Regiment and heard many such gems. As a recruit, I heard a Sergeant inform us on the rifle range that we had thirty seconds to fire off five rounds at a target – " 'An" remember . . . thirty seconds ain't many minutes a-gooin'."

Once, I heard a fellow complaining about the local Council: "They collect yer rates but they dow dew nothin' for yer. Down our street there's 'oles in the road two foot 'igh."

I was watching a fellow planting seed potatoes one Good Friday morning: "Yo' got ter put 'em in the right distance ter get the most out of 'em . . . some will put 'em in too nigh apart."

Here is another example. A motorist asked the way to get to Cradley Heath and received the following directions: "Yo' want ter goo straight along back weer yo' cum from till yo' cum to a boozer called the Black Swan. We call it the Mucky Duck. About 'arf a mile afore yew cum to it yo' tern right. No . . . I'm wrong, yo' tern left, that's right. No . . . no, wait a bit. It's a orkard pierce ter get to is Cradley. If I wus goin' ter Cradley I wouldn't start from 'ere."

Sounds a bit Irish, doesn't it?

During the Industrial Revolution, many 'sons of Erin' came to the Black Country to put their muscle into the heavy industries, thinking, no doubt, that half a loaf was far better than no potatoes. I often wonder . . . did they bring something else with them beside their brawn? I have found that nowhere in Great Britain is there a greater similarity of the humour of the Irish and that of the Black Countryman.

BILLY RUSSELL.

When a man's busy, why leisure
Strikes him as wonderful pleasure;
But when at leisure is he,
Straightaway, he wants to be busy.

Blackcountry author.

A Coseley man on Home Guard duty during World War II:

"Halt."

The approaching figure stopped obediently and gave his name and business.

"Where's yo're identity card?"

"I've gone an' left it at wum."

"Oh, arr'. Well, doe yo' shift from theer till yo've bin an' fetched it."

* * *

The beer in the officers' mess not being up to standard it was sent out to the men. Meeting a sergeant of the company, an officer enquired what the beer was like.

"Just right, sir," said the sergeant.

"Did the men find it good?"

"Just right," the man said again.

"What exactly do you mean, sergeant, by just right?"

"Well, sir. It's like this. If it 'ad bin any worse we couldn't a drunk it . . . an' if it 'ad bin any better we shouldn't a 'ad the chance."

* * *

In the trenches, the mail had been distributed.

"Why, Joe, there ay ony writin' on the sheet o' paeper yo've just took out o' that envelope. I thought it was a letter from yer wife."

"So it is, yer fule, but doe yer know as we doe spake?"

* * *

N.C.O. drilling local territorials:

"When I gives the order 'about turn,' yo' turns round on yer right 'eel an' left toe, an' you' ends up with yer front at the back."

* * *

Sergeant to new recruit: "What's the first movement to 'bout face?"

Recruit: "When the command is given yer advance the right foot to the rear."

8

On a quiet stretch of the front in the First World War, the colonel was addressing men of the South Staffordshire Regiment:

"Now, men. We want more action on this front. To encourage competition amongst you fellows, I will myself reward any soldier who captures a German alive from today with two pounds for every prisoner taken."

That night, Eynuk and Eli are on guard together.

"Eh, Eli, wake up."

"What's up, Eynuk?"

"Tell me, ower kid, dun yo' think that officer bloke this mornin' was tellin' the truth, that 'e'll pay us two quid for every German we cop alive?"

"Cos 'e was! Yo' know them officers, they'm all flush."

"Well, doe yo' tell onybody, mate, but theer's ten thousand quid's wuth a-cummin' over that field."

*　　*　　*

Sergeant: " 'Tension, front face, and attend to roll call. As many as are present say 'ere, an' as many as is not present say absent."

*　　*　　*

A very young Guards officer was chatting to a group of ex-Service men at a post-war dinner. Emphasising with what precision they had to march and keep in step, he gave them an illustration: "Left, right, left right, left, right . . ."

"Ah," said a one-time ranker of the Staffordshires, "when we cum back from forin service we was reviewed by one o' yo' Guards an' yo' shud 'a' seen us march. Left, right, jingle, jingle, left, right, jingle, jingle . . . "

"What's the jingle, jingle?" interrupted the officer.

"O, that was we medals."

ARMY

The new recruit was unable to grasp even the most elementary details of drill.

"Whoever gid yo' a job in peacetime, I cor think," said the sergeant. "Per'aps yo' never 'ad a job?"

"Oh, I 'ad a job all rite," the recruit told him, "but I dey kip it long. I was in a ty factory, an' 'ad to pack ty soldiers an' I got the sack for puttin' too many sergeants in the boxes."

* * *

The sergeant was giving rifle drill. Blank cartridges were loaded and the men stood at 'ready.'

"Now," ordered the sergeant, "Fire at will."

One recruit hesitated and lowered his rifle: " 'Scuse me, Sarge, but I'se ony just jined the platoon. Which o' the blokes is Will?"

* * *

"You 'orrible soldier . . . why 'aven't you pressed your trousers?"

"Tay my fault, sarge. I 'ad 'em folded under me mattress all right. But I'm a light sleeper."

If thou would'st view the Black Country aright,
Go see it from Dudley's Grey Keep at night.

———————

In Wednesbury town, a town whose name
Is coupled with its cocking fame,
Was yearly held by custom's right,
A wake where colliers met to fight,
Where bulls were baited, torn, abused,
And dogs were killed, which much amused
Those sturdy knights of coal and hammer
Who scoff at peace and joy at clamour.

———————

When Satan stood on Brierley Hill and far
around him gazed,
He said: "I never more shall feel at hell's
fierce flames amazed."

ANIMALS

"Weer wun yer when yer dey goo out last night?"

"I went to Tip'n to buy a dog a bloke gid me."

"Oh, ah! It is a good 'un?"

"It ay auf. Well, I'll tell thee. W'en I got wum with 'im, I took 'im down the backyard an' cheined 'im up wi' a bit o' rope."

"Did yer? I'll cum and see 'im."

"Ah, yo' cum. Well, to goo on wi' me tael, any'ow, w'en I went ter see 'im this mornin' 'e was theer all rite–gone."

*　　*　　*

"Is your father in, my boy?"

"No, 'e's in the pigsty, clanin' the pigs out. Yo'll see which is faether, 'e's got 'is 'at on."

*　　*　　*

The mongrel dog was of such good appearance that its owner took it to a local dog show.

"Take that dog out," shouted one of the judges. "His legs are too short."

"What's the matter with 'is legs," retorted the owner. "They raeches the ground, doe 'em?"

*　　*　　*

" 'ullo, Tom, 'ow bin yer? I ay sid yer for a wik or tew. Yo' doe look tew good."

"No, an' 'I doe feel it nayther. I ay 'ad anny slep for a fortnit."

" 'ow is it yer cor slape? Got a paen or summat?"

"No, I ay got anny paen, but me naeber's got a dog an' 'e barks all nite."

"Well, yo' con soon put that rite. Yo' buy 'is dog, an' then it ull be 'im as cor slape."

*　　*　　*

A man advertised a horse for sale, stressing that it was well bred.

Said a prospective purchaser: "You say the horse is well bred; who is he by?"

"What do you mean, by? He's by his bloody self, of course."

12

ANIMALS

Two boys seeing a Dachshund for the first time:
"Ain't 'is legs worn down low?"
"They bay auf. I specs 'e's dun a lot o' warkin' in 'is time."

* * *

"Weer's that bull terrier o' yourn, Bill? I ay sid 'im laetly."
"O, 'e's jed."
"Jed? Wen did 'e die? Wot was the matter wi' 'im?"
"Yo' know as aythin' 'e sid movin' 'e started ter fight it? Well, I was in a timber yard wi' 'im one day, an' 'e started on the circler saw, but 'e only 'ad one round."

* * *

A dirty and dishevelled man dashed up to a boy in the street. "Have you seen a lorry load of pigs go by?" he demanded.
"No," said the boy, " 'ave yo' dropped off? "

* * *

Said a witness, asked if she was present in the party yard when the scrap took place: "Well I was, an' I wort. I just went out ter fetch our dog in, as 'e allus bites people's legs w'en there's a row gooin' on, an' they doe altogether like it."

* * *

Strangers had called at the house and the mongrel dog was looking menacing. The woman of the house shook a warning finger at the animal: "Now yo' stay there. Now yo' shift!"

* * *

"Mother," enquired a small child, "do dogs go to heaven when they die?"
"No, they don't go to heaven."
"Well, do cats?"
"No; no animals go to heaven, only good little boys and girls and grown-ups when they die."

13

ANIMALS

"Well," said the child, "cows don't go either, so I suppose when we get to heaven and want any milk, we shall have to go to the naughty place for it."

*   *   *

With the prospect of selling a hack to the Bishop, a horse dealer sought advice.

" 'Ow dun yer tork to a bishop, Joe? I never met one afore."

"Oh, it ay nuthin' tew worry yer 'ead over. Yo' address 'im as 'My Lord,' an' if yo' get a sootable opportunity, quote a bit o' scripture; they like that."

When the horses were submitted, the Bishop picked the one he liked best. "But I don't like his hocks," said he.

"My Lord," said the dealer. "Yo' con tek it from me, there's nothin' the matter with 'is 'ocks, or 'is ass, or anythin' that is 'is."

*   *   *

A man gave his son a £1 to buy a horse at Bromsgrove Fair, then had second thought and called him back:

" 'Ere"s another tew an' six, yo' might as well bring a good 'un."

*   *   *

Two local tatters went to the Tipton horse fair and bought a couple of horses. After putting them into their field, they were about to go home when one said to the other: " 'Eh! We ay decided which is yourn an' which un is mine."

"Yo'm right," said the other. "I'll cut off half the tael o' mine."

He did this, but later the local children came and cut off half the tail of the other horse. Next day the two men called for their horses.

"Look at this," said the one. "What can we dew now?"

"I'll tell yo' what," said the other. "Yo' 'ave the black un an' I'll 'ave the white un!"

*   *   *

A couple of Black Country men invested all their savings in a greyhound. Despite every care, it always came in last in every race. Finally, fed up with the expense of keeping the animal, they decided to get rid of it and they took it down to the canal.

"Sholl we chuck 'im in, Olf?"

"No," said the other disgustedly. "Let's just walk away an' leave 'im."

14

BOASTING

"Thee cosn't ride a bike," said the pillion passenger to his friend who had just acquired a motor cycle. "Why, yo'm a wobblin' all over the shop."

"Who cor ride? There's two lights a-comin' down the road. Yo' see me goo right between 'em."

*　　*　　*

Two friends walking along the canal, the one broad and tall, the other rather undersized. They had an argument and the stronger of the pair threatened for "two pins" he would fling the little man on to the opposite bank.

"I bet yer auf a dollar as yo' cor do it," said the little man, and the bet was accepted.

The big man picked up his companion, swung him round a few times and let him go–dropping him into the middle of the canal.

"Yo' owe me auf a dollar," he gulped as he bobbed out of the water.

"I doe," said the big man. "I dey say as I could do it fust time."

" 'Er sed 'er wud an' 'er cud an' 'er shud, but 'er doe."

When two friends were returning from work together, one boasted of a wonderful cat he had at home, and of its capacity as a 'mouser'. The other, impressed, decided that after he had 'ad his tay and claned 'imself up, he would call and have a look at it. When he arrived he found the cat purring away, lying full length before the blazing fire.

Presently a number of mice came from under or adjacent to the fireplace. The cat took not the slightest notice.

"I thought yo' tode me 'er was a good mouser," said the visitor. "Why 'er doe tek any notice on 'em."

"Of course 'er does, yer fule," said his friend. "Them bin our mice; yo' wait till some strangers come, then yo'll see."

*　　*　　*

A family man with 15 children was boasting to a fellow workman about the very fine celery he had grown on his allotment: "If yo'll call some time, I'll gie yer a stick."

15

BOASTING

Duly calling at the allotment, the friend was handed a 'stick', but demurred at having it for nothing. "Doe bother about that," he was told. "I doe waent anythin'. Gie the kids a penny a piece, that ull do me."

*　*　*

Two lads were looking at a police notice showing a man wanted for murder.

"That's my faether," said one.

"Go on," scoffed the other. "Yo'm allus a braggin'."

*　*　*

"What meks that 'en o' yorn cackle so loud, ower kid?"

"Oh, they've just laid a foundation stone across the road an' 'er wants t'other fowl ter think 'er did it."

*　*　*

"Joe, I ay got ony swate paes in me allotment, an' I'd buy some o' yore sids if they'm quick growers."

"They ay auf. All yo've got to doo is put the sades in an' jump clear."

*　*　*

" 'ers tall, is ower wench. Yo' con tell, 'er 'as ter stond on a chaer to put 'er 'at on."

*　*　*

Two Black Country men on a works outing to London found themselves in the Jewish quarter. Seeing a sign in Yiddish, one said: "What's it say on that sign?" His mate, a member of the local town band, replied: "I cor tell yer wot it says, but if I 'ad me tromboon I cud play it."

BOOZING

Two colliers in London for a cup-tie ended up in Piccadilly very much the worse for drink. They were looking at the lights and got separated, with the result that one of them found himself down in the Underground. After staggering around for some time he regained the open air and, luckily, walked slap into his friend.

"Weer in th' 'ell an yo' bin?" he was asked.

"I got down some bloke's cellar," he was told. "An' I'll tell yo' summat. 'E's got the best set o' trains I ever sid."

*　　*　　*

"Drinking," said a young man to his girl, "meks yo' beautiful."

"But darling, I haven't been drinking."

"No," he agreed, "but I 'ave."

*　　*　　*

"If yo'd abin sober yo'd a 'ad sense enoo to know as yo' was drunk."

*　　*　　*

The son of an innkeeper was given £10 with which to purchase a parrot as an attraction for the bar. Instead of buying a parrot he lost the money at the races and was forced to come home empty handed.

"Father," said he, "it was like this: I bought the parrot and was on my way home with him, and he kept saying, 'Does your father carry on with the barmaid? Does your father carry on with the barmaid?' so I wrung his blinkin' neck."

"Quite right, my boy; quite right. We don't want any of them sort of parrots here."

*　　*　　*

"I reckon that beer as I've 'ad to-nite ay much cop. There's no strength in it. Why, I doe know as I've 'ad any," remarked a man to his pal as they walked home. To reach his cottage, he had to cross a narrow plank over a stream. Falling off the plank into the water, he remarked, "That beer wor as bad as I thort it was."

17

BOOZING

The pub passage was draughty and full of smoke. Just inside was a baby carriage in which an infant was squealing lustily. After a while the mother came out of the bar, wiping her lips. Shaking the pram angrily, she said to the babe: "If yo' do hush up, I shor bring yo' again."

*   *   *

Said an old man in a mood of reminiscence: "These bay like the good owd times when we used to goo boozin' an' cum wum at one or tew in the mornin' an' stop outside a 'ouse an' knock up the ode woman an' call up at the winder: Ay, missus, cum an' pick yourn out o' we."

*   *   *

Too drunk to continue his homeward journey, a man drove his horse and trap into a field while he slept off the effects under a hedge.

When he woke up he saw the trap but no horse.

"If I'm me," said he, "I've lost a 'oss. If I ain't me, I've found a trap."

*   *   *

Three men determined to have a good time round the pubs, decided that one of the party should act as banker and do the paying out, on the understanding that there should be a settling up at the end of the evening. They were outside their last port of call at closing time.

"Well, 'ow do we stond?" said the temporary chancellor of the exchequer.

"God knows," said one of the party. "But 'ere goes; I'm off wum."

*   *   *

A proud father and his friends had made a good job of "wetting the babby's yed" at the local pub.

"Mind yo'," said the father. "Er ony weighed fower pound."

"Sh'all right," assured his friend. "I dey weigh as much as that when I wus born."

"Thas terrible, ode mate. Did yer live?"

"Corsh I did. Why, yo' ought ter shee me now."

18

"Gie me a pint o' auf an' auf, Miss, an' put the mild on top, I waents ter drink that fust."

"Yo' doe look too well this mornin', ow'er kid," said one workman to another as they commenced their day's work.

"No, I doe feel too well, nither. I 'ad a bet last nite as to wether ode Bill could drink the most beer or me, an' it ay decided yet. When we finished up at fower this mornin' we was level peggins, so we've got to start agen to-nite to settle it."

* * *

Two drunks were scrapping in the street on a pouring wet night. After a quarter of an hour, during which the bigger man was astride the weaker, pummelling him for all he was worth, he said: "Hast 'ad anew now?"

"No, I ay," gasped the underdog, defiantly.

"Well, theest best cum on top for a bit. I'm gettin' bloody soaked up 'ere."

* * *

Returning home from a gathering at his local club, a somewhat canned husband was asked by his wife what he had got under his arm.

"Oh, I won it in a draw."

"That's illegal."

"Is it? When they gid it me I thought it was a turkey."

* * *

"Yo'm lookin' cheerful, ay yer aer' kid?"

"Ar, ween got extermination up ut our pub."

"Wa' dust mean?"

"They'm open an' 'our after they'm shut."

* * *

An exchange of experiences on the morning after the night before:

" 'Ow did you get wum, Bill?"

"Oh, I tumbled down a time or two, but I got wum all right at last. How did you get on?"

"Oh, I was all right till some fule trod on me onds goin' up our entry."

BOOZING

The publican was noted for giving short measure:

" 'Ow many kegs o' beer dun yo' sell 'ere in a wik?"

"About thirty."

"Ah ... well, I con tell yer 'ow yo' con sell sixty."

"How?"

"Fill up the bleedin' glasses!"

*　　*　　*

A policeman, seeing a man who had obviously spent a merry evening, fumbling at a door with his latch-key, enquired if he was all right.

"Yes, thanks," said the man, hiccuping.

Two hours later the policeman came by again on his round and saw the man still there, sitting on the step.

"Are you sure you're all right, sir?" he enquired again.

"Yes, I'm all right, offisher. Them in theer wouldn't answer the door when I knocked, so I'm makin' 'em wait."

*　　*　　*

A reveller who had had one over the eight wandered into a milk bar and asked for a pint of beer. The girl gave him a large glass of milk.

"Ay, miss," he said. "Doe yo' know 'ow ter pull? This 'ere beer's all froth."

*　　*　　*

Fed up with her husband for not bringing home his wages from the ironworks, a wife traced him to the pub, where he was surrounded by companions. She gave him a good ticking off in front of everybody. Eventually, as she paused for breath, her husband stood up.

"Would any other lady or gentleman," he asked, "like to put a penny in the slot before I remove the instrument?"

BOOZING

Village nurse trying to persuade an old lady to take liquid food. "Will you take some Bovril?"

"Na, I could'na tak it."

"Perhaps you would like a cup of tea?"

"Na, I could'na tak that either."

"Well, what about a glass of whisky?"

"Aye," responded the invalid, "Mak it strong an' make me tak it."

* * *

On a very bright moonlight night, a man on his way home with a friend along the 'cut' after a night at the local suddenly asked his pal what that round thing was he could see "down there."

"That's the mune, ye fule."

"Tay, 'is it? Well, what the 'ell brings us up 'ere then?"

* * *

A drunk walking down the street, dragging behind him a length of clothes line, enquired of a constable; "Offisher, can yo' tell me weer I con find the invisible man?"

In order to humour him, the officer asked what he wanted the invisible man for.

"Well," said the drunk. "It's like this 'ere, I've got 'is dog."

* * *

A small boy entered a public house and asked for a quart of beer to be put into a can he had brought.

"How old are you?" enquired the barman.

"I'm ten."

"I'm afraid I can't serve you, then."

"Cor yer? Well send somebody what con."

* * *

Pressed to have another drink before going home, a man said: "Ah, well, perhaps I 'ull. We'm goin' ter 'ave 'addocks for supper, an' it allus mak's me thirsty."

21

BOOZING

A reveller returning home, was stepping first on the kerb and occasionally with a foot in the gutter. "Yo' want ter tek it easy," said a friend. "Doe yo' know you'm drunk?"

"I 'om, 'om I? I'm glad yo' tode me, I thought I'd gone lame."

*   *   *

Asked by his daughter why he had given up drinking, a former heavy tippler replied: "It's like this 'ere. The last time I cum 'ome tight yer mother was waitin' up fer me, an' I saw two on 'er, an' that cured me."

*   *   *

"I'm fed up o' yo're drinkin'." a woman raved to her husband. "You'm always at the pub. I'm agooin' to the ironmongers to get some chaien to chaien yer up."

"Doe goo ter that expense, me wench; a bit o' cotton ull do fer that job," he told her.

*   *   *

A workman had gone home ill, and had been advised by the young personnel officer to send for a doctor. "Doctor be damned," said the man's mate. "If yo'd tode 'im to tek a couple o' quaerts o' ode aele when 'e got wum, 'e'd abin back at waerk in the mornin'."

"Weer bin I gooin'? I ay gooin' noweer, I'm a-comin' back."

The old-fashioned public house had been completely modernised.

"S'all right," commented one customer of many years. "But I miss the spitoons."

"Arr," said the landlord. "An' yo missed 'em w'en we 'ad 'em an' all."

*   *   *

"I always take a little water with my wine," said one guest to another, as the decanter was being passed round. "It brings out the flavour."

22

BOOZING

"Cum an' 'ave a drop o' beer wi' me," said a man to an out-of-work friend.

"Well I ay 'ad ony for a month; I'll just 'ave a mouthful."

"Doe yo' be greedy, I'm ony gooin' ter stond yer a pint."

*   *   *

A befuddled man, boarding a bus one Saturday night, asked a man next to whom he sat if he had seen him get on.

"Yes," he was told.

"Dun yo' know me?"

"No, nor doe want to."

"Then, if yo' doe know me, 'ow dun yo' know it was me as got on?"

*   *   *

"A lot o' drink's no good to nobody. I know our Jack doe drink at night' or 'e wudn't be so thirsty in a mornin' when 'e waekes up."

*   *   *

A man who was limping badly was asked what ailed him.

"Oh, I get these 'ere rumatics."

"Well," said his friend. "Have you ever tried goin' wi'out beer?"

"Well, to tell yer the truth, I 'ave thunk about it, but I cor maek up me mind whether to be wi'out beer or wi'out me rumatics."

*   *   *

Two drunks squaring up to a fight, watched by their mates. Said one: "Tew on yer ode 'im back. One ull be enough to ode me."

*   *   *

Wife was fetched to see her husband lying on the roadside.

" 'E ay drunk," she pronounced. "I sid 'im move."

*   *   *

Definition of 'pit beer' – "Chuck three grains o' malt in the cut and drink as much as yo' like."

BOOZING

" I wish as beer was auf the price."

"Arr . . . An' every pint as big as a gasometer."

*   *   *

Two colliers went to another town to see their football team play in a cup match. Afterwards they had a meal and more than a few drinks.

"When we gets whum," said one, "I sholl buy our collery."

"Yo' wo," said the other, "because I sholl."

A heated argument developed.

"It's no use yo' argifyin' 'cos there's nothin' to stop me buyin' it."

"There is," replied his mate, " 'cos I shor sell it yer."

*   *   *

After many year of drinking together, the son arrived home late one night without his father.

"Where's yer dad?" his mother asked.

"Well," said the son, "we cum owt the boozer and took the short way along the cut. All on a sudden me dad shouted: 'It ay auf ruff on this pavement. Ah'm gonner walk in the 'oss road.' After that I dey see 'im agen!"

CHURCH AND CHAPEL

The preacher had been speaking on the prophets for some forty minutes and there were signs of unrest amongst his congregation.

"And now," he asked, "where shall we find a place for Elijah?"

A voice from the back of the chapel shouted: "There's a sate 'ere, cos I'm agooin' wum."

*   *   *

A minister on his round of calls, came across an old sinner poring over the Bible. "Glad to see you're improving in your old age, John."

"Me improvin'?" was the reply. "We'm got a litter o' pups an' I'm just lookin for names to gie 'em."

*   *   *

Asked if he ever attended church, a man said that he had been twice in his life. Once they chucked water in his face; the next time they tied him up so tight to a 'ooman as 'e 'ad never bin able ter break away.

"Arr, and the next time," chuckled his questioner, "yo'll ayther 'ave dirt thrown at yer, or yo'll be berned ter jeth."

*   *   *

Closing remarks of an old-time local preacher, much given to ranting:

"My brethren, tonite we've gid the Devil a rough time. We've 'it 'im all over, above the belt and below the belt. Tripped 'im up and we've knocked 'im down, and we've charged into 'im a good 'un. But doe forget, 'e'll be about termorrer at 'is dirty work agen, so be ready w'en 'e gets on the prowl an' be sure an' 'ave no truck with 'im, an' then, plase God, we'll 'ave another goo at 'im next Sunday."

*   *   *

Given a talking parrot, a rather prim lady shocked at the bird's language, kept it quiet on Sundays by placing a dark cover over the cage. One day, seeing the chapel minister approaching, she rushed to cover the bird. As she did so it said: "Bloody short wik, ay it?"

*   *   *

An old chapel had been sold to a garage proprietor and turned into a repair shop. The walls were still decorated with a few appropriate texts, one of which read: "This is the House of God."

CHURCH AND CHAPEL

A customer who considered he had been overcharged for repairs to his car, added to the text so that it read: "This is the House of God, and thou hast made it a den of thieves."

"Theer yo' bin, it allus sometimes never 'appens what's least expected most."

A Nonconformist leader was offering up thanks to the Almighty for the safe return of the minister and his wife from a holiday trip.

"O, Lord," he said, "we thank Thee for bringing our pastor safely home, and his dear wife, too, O Lord, for Thou preservest both man and beast."

* * *

A commemoration window was placed in a church in memory of a man and his wife who had been great benefactors to the district. Parishioners had been invited to view the window.

A man, stopping in front of a stained glass representation of Moses and Aaron, said to his wife: "It's very nice, but it doe much fature the ode couple, doo it?"

* * *

An elderly man asked to establish proof of his age, called on the vicar to obtain a certificate of baptism from the church register.

"How old do you say you are?"

"Seventy, vicar."

"Good gracious. I'm only sixty, and you look even younger than I do."

"Arr . . . But yo' see, I've alus lived a careful life. Never got drunk nor med a pig o' meself in the 'atin' line."

* * *

Writing out a baptism certificate, the vicar hesitated over the date. "Let me see," he asked the mother, "Is this the tenth?"

"Oh, dear, no, vicar! We'm ony bin married three 'ears."

CHURCH AND CHAPEL

A vicar was curious as to why a once regular member of his congregation had ceased to attend church.

"Not Atheism, I hope?"

"No, worse nor that–rheumatism."

* * *

After a long wait, the cottage door was finally opened to the young rector. "See 'ere," said the woman. "It's washin' day at our 'ouse, and I'm too busy ter waste time gabbin' ter yo'. Anyrode, if it's religion yo'm called about, we'em sooted."

* * *

A man who travelled to and from his work every weekday by train, fell into a doze one Sunday during the church service. He was barely half awake when the plate came round. The sidesman gave him a nudge, whereupon he shouted: "Season, season, you fool."

* * *

The chapel preacher was describing how, although there was scriptural authority that the devil was in chains, the reach of that Prince of Darkness was very extensive.

"Brother Jones," he said, "If you commit a sin, the devil can reach you; the same applies to you, brothers so-and-so" – calling the congregation by name.

"Well, as far as I con see," said one brother in a loud voice, "if he con reach all that fur the bugger may as well be loose."

* * *

A vicar remarked to a boy who was behaving badly. "You are better fed than taught."

"Yes," said the boy, "Ah feeds meself."

* * *

A local preacher was talking in his sermon about Daniel, and explained thus his miraculous deliverance from the lions.

"The rason they day ate owd Daniel was, 'e was all backbone and grit."

27

CHURCH AND CHAPEL

A Bishop in holiday attire came upon a shepherd in charge of his flock somewhere in the wilds. He enquired of the shepherd how many sheep his flock contained and was told they numbered one hundred and forty.

The Bishop then remarked that he was also a shepherd, but that the flock of which he was in charge consisted of over forty thousand sheep.

The shepherd was suitably impressed. An expatriate from the Black Country, he said: "Bost me, gaffer! Yo' must be 'ellish busy in the lambing season."

"Wot am yer torkin' about? Cum down out o' the clouds, yo'm disturbin' the birds."

A man was roundly cursing his dog, when he was approached by a stranger and told firmly that such language would not be tolerated in those parts.

"An' who the 'ell dun yo' think yo' am?'

"I am the Rector of this parish."

"Well, yo'm got a dom'd good job. Mind and behave yerself an' kip it!"

*   *   *

"I want to call at Mrs. Smith's shop," said a small girl on the way home from church with her mother.

"You can't call there. It's Sunday."

"But I want to. I want a banana."

"On a Sunday? Certainly not. Don't you know that children who buy things on Sunday won't go to heaven?"

"I don't want to go to heaven. I want to go to Smith's."

*   *   *

A mischievous son of an elderly, short-sighted pastor gummed two pages of the Bible together in the section from which his father had chosen to read the lesson. He read:

"And Judas went out and hanged himself, and his bowels gushed forth and the lot fell upon Matthias."

CHURCH AND CHAPEL

The new vicar was suspicious when he saw the verger abstract a pound coin from the collection and put it in his pocket. He asked for an explanation.

"Oh," said the verger, "that's all right, vicar. We've 'ad that quid for 'ears; it's only a ticer as we leads off with every Sunday."

*　　*　　*

A Bishop came out to his car after a dinner party and found his chauffeur not quite sober.

"Drunk again, Jonathan?" he said sadly, and the latter promptly retorted:

"Jump in, me lord, an' nobody ull notice."

*　　*　　*

An old-fashioned ranting lay preacher was occupying an elevated closed-in Chapel pulpit, and wildly gesticulating. A little boy in the congregation plucked nervously at his mother's coat. "What shon we doo if 'e gets out?" he whispered.

*　　*　　*

The new curate paused to speak to a group of workmen gathered outside a public house.

"Shall I see you men next Sunday?" he asked. "I sincerely hope so."

"Yo' con cum if yer like," said one. "An' what abaht yo' bringin' the beer? The pigeon raece starts off the w'ite nobs, abaht ten."

*　　*　　*

Asked by the new vicar if they had Matins at the church, the verger replied: "No, vicar, we 'as linoleum all down the hile."

*　　*　　*

"My mom's very bad with a floatin' kidney," a woman told the vicar. "Dun yo' mind prayin' next Sunday for it to get better?"

"Oh, I couldn't do that; it would sound so ridiculous," said the vicar.

"Well," she said crossly. "Yo' prayed for loose livers last wik, an' I doe see much difference."

"What was the vicar sayin' last Sunday about Lot's wife?" asked one girl of another. "What did 'e mean by 'Remember Lot's wife.' What did 'er dew?"

"O, 'er looked back," said her friend, "an' 'er wus terned into a pillar o' salt, an' serve 'er right, the fast madam."

*   *   *

Speaking in his sermon on the marvels of nature, a vicar mentioned that every blade of grass is a sermon. Cutting his lawn the next morning, he was seen by a member of his congregation, who remarked: "That's right, vicar, cut your sermons short."

"Look weer they'm a-gooin'. Why, they'm gone the way as they ought ter cum back."

The vicar went to London to buy a new banner for the Sunday School children to carry in a procession at Christmas time. Having forgotten both the size required and the wording, he asked for a reply-paid wire to be sent. Calling for the reply, he was heartily congratulated by the post office assistant.

The reply read: "Unto us a child is born. 12 ft. x 9 ft."

*   *   *

Promoting conversation, the visiting parson said: I notice, Mrs. Jones, you've been making pastry this morning."

"What makes you think that, vicar?"

"Oh, I can always tell that by the nails."

"Well, you'm wrong; that's last wik's. I allus maekes me paestry on a Friday."

*   *   *

"Did yo' 'ear our Joe a-snorin' doorin' the sermon?"

"I day auf. It was disgraceful. It woke me up."

The vicar, fastidious about his diet, was taking supper with a family of parishioners. The son of the house, who was going though a phase of swearing, was promised a bicycle if he behaved himself during the meal.

Several dishes were brought to the table, all of which on some ground or another the vicar refused.

The boy could stand it no longer: "Bicycle or no bloody bicycle," he burst out. "Boil the bugger an egg."

* * *

A Gornal Wood couple were having their child christened at Dudley.

"Was this child born in wedlock?" enquired the Reverend.

"Noa, it worn't," said the man. "It were born in Gornal Ud."

* * *

Persuaded to go to church for the first time in her life, an Old Hill woman put on a worn white apron to cover a shabby dress. When they got to the singing of the hymn, Holy, Holy, Holy, she shouted: "I doe care if it is 'oly, it's clane."

* * *

Coming out of church, a woman remarked, "I don't like the preacher, I don't like the church, I don't like the people in it, and' I didn't like the service."

"Well," said her little boy, "what can yer expect for a penny?"

* * *

Chided by the vicar for going to the public house after service, the verger retorted that he always had a thirst after righteousness.

* * *

"Our minister knows what 'e's a torkin' about w'en 'e says in 'is sermon as 'ow the devil knows just w'en ter tempt yer," said a housewife. "S'never I gits me 'ands in the dough, me nose begins to itch."

* * *

Asking a country Rector why he wore a violet stole, a Bishop got the reply: "A parson should always be 'inviolate'."

"This an' better might do . . . this an wuss 'ull never do."

DEATH AND FUNERALS

Two mates who had been to a fellow workman's funeral got to worrying about their own fate.

"I'd gie all I've got" said one, "If I could know the plaece wheer I wus a-gooin' ter die."

"What good 'ud that dew, onyroad?"

"Well, I'd tek bloody good care not to goo theer, that's what."

* * *

"I dey know yore Jim was jed."

"Oh, arr! If 'e'd a-lived till termorrer 'ed a bin jed a fortnit."

* * *

The pub 'regulars' were discussing some of the old curators of Wednesbury cemetery.

"O'd Bill was the wust," said one, " 'e wus so saft, 'e used ter tek a roll call every night ter see that nobody 'ad got out."

* * *

In spite of a period of convalescence at the seaside, a Black Country woman had died shortly after returning home. An old friend was taken by the husband to see her as she lay in the house.

"Doe 'er look beautiful?" said the friend.

"Well," said the husband, "an' so 'er ought. 'Er's just 'ad a fortnit at Blackpool, ay 'er?"

* * *

"I was glad as my mother dey die till 'er 'ad 'er Christmas gift from the church," one woman told another. "The vicar sent 'er a small loaf an' a chemise. I took 'em to 'er an' 'er was that plased. 'Mother, I says, no one shor wear this chemise but yo'. I'll lay yer out in it,' I says. An' I did. Wor it nice for 'er to tek 'er gift with 'er?"

* * *

A lady was ordering a wreath for the funeral of a well-known resident: "I expect," she said to the florist, "You've got a lot of orders for this funeral?"

"Yes, mum. But not nearly so many as we sholl 'ave when yo'er ode man goes, 'e's that popular."

32

DEATH AND FUNERALS

A parson asked to conduct a funeral service read on the order of service: "After the service the congregation will walk round the coffin."

Thinking this rather crude, he altered the reading and read out–"After the service the congregation will pass round the bier."

"Poor owd feller, 'e wor one o' the wust at 'is best, 'e wor. Ah, well, let's 'ope 'e's gone weer we think 'e ain't.

Notice in undertaker's window:

"Why walk about in misery when you can be buried in comfort for a few pounds?"

*   *   *

It was the young curate's first experience of a funeral service. After the commitment in the cemetery he felt that he should try to make himself agreeable to the mourners, so he sidled up to them as they were taking their last look at the coffin. Making conversation, he rubbed his hands together, looked round and observed: "The cemetery's filling up nicely, isn't it?"

*   *   *

"We wants a bit o' portry to finish up with," said a bereaved widow to the clerk at the newspaper counter, after furnishing the other necessary details for the notice. After taking some time to choose a verse, she said to her friend:

"What dun yo' think o' this 'un?"

"I think it's luvverly."

"Well, then, I s'pose we shall 'ave to 'ave it, but 'e was a bad blighter to me!"

*   *   *

Better late . . .

"I shor 'ave the wife's funeral for a wik, as I allus said I'd see she 'ad a nice quiet wik when I could arrange it."

*   *   *

At a funeral service in a village chapel, when a young man was about to be buried, the hymn, "Now the labourer's task is o'er" was sung. Greatly annoyed, the mother said it wur fair, as 'er son was a clerk.

33

DEATH AND FUNERALS

A woman who had just buried her no-good husband went to stay with her brother, a farmer. He remarked what grand growing weather it was, and that everything in the ground was coming up this year.

"Good Lord," said his sister, thoroughly alarmed, "I hope not."

* * *

A man who had just buried his wife was asked by the undertaker to ride in the same coach as his mother-in-law.

"I'll dew it just to oblige yer," he said, "but doe forget you'm agoin' to spile me dey."

* * *

Consoling a dead man's sister, a friend of the family went on to express surprise at the suddenness of her brother's death. "Yes," she said. "It was a great surprise to us as well, because at grandfather's funeral three weeks ago he was the jolliest of the lot."

* * *

"Yo've 'eard about Missis Jones a-dyin', ay yer?"

"O, arr! 'Ers bein' buried terday. Our Sairey was there w'en 'er died, but they dey ask 'er to lay 'er out an' 'er'd knowed 'er from a kid. A bit 'ard, we thought."

* * *

A successful self-made Black Country merchant took a last look into the grave of a one-time competitor; "Ah," he soliloquised, " 'e ain't died wuth much. Wait till they see my will in the paeper, that ull mak 'em sit up an' tek notice."

* * *

"Not much pleasure in gooin' ter funerals now," remarked a bearer, attending the funeral of a friend. "It's different when you'm young."

34

Ali Scriven's wife was dying and all the relatives were round the bed.

"Doe yo' forget our Ali," she said weakly, "as Mrs. Jones as lives in Grainger's Lane owes us twenty-five bob for groceries out'n the shop."

"Lissen at 'er," said Ali. "Sensible to the last."

"An' do yo' forget neither, as we owes ode Fellows two quid fer coal."

"Ah," said Ali. "Now 'er's awanderin'."

*　　*　　*

A woman's third husband came across the tombstone of his two predecessors in the local cemetery: "Ay," he soliloquised. "If 'er 'ad only a-married me when I wanted 'er to I should a bin first name on that stone."

*　　*　　*

An undertaker who made a point of allowing special terms to poor people, became a candidate for the Town Council. A woman being canvassed for her vote said: "I'll vote for 'im. 'E did me a good turn once ... buried my ode mon cheap."

"I'm that worried, I wishes I could waik up jed every mornin' o' me life."

Tom went to see his dying father. After awhile the old chap said to his son: "Pass me my trousers off the brass knob at the foot o' the bed." Tom obeyed and the old man reached into the pockets and eventually produced a two shilling piece. "This is all the money I've got," he said. "I want yo' to 'ave it and I want you to do this for me. Yo' know the Red Lion in Cemetery Road? Well, when they tek me to the cemetery ask the undertaker ter stop at the Red Lion. Yo' goo in ... an' leave me outside like yo' always did!"

"If yo've laid 'im out yo' dun know the end on 'im."

DEATH AND FUNERALS

They were discussing the latest widow in the street.

"They tell me she's got fifty pounds for 'im, she insured 'im so."

"She maekes out 'e wort worth moor than ten to 'er."

"Doe tell me! Look what the buryin's cost 'em. An' 'er's gone an' bought two new pigs and put 'em in black (the family), an' 'er's about startin' a shop. The poor ode feller was worth more to 'er jed than livin'."

* * *

Following the cremation of her husband, a widow had the ashes placed in an egg-timer.

Asked for an explanation, she said: "Well 'e dey dew ony waerk w'en 'e was alive, an' I'm agooin' to see as 'e maks hisself useful now 'e's jed."

* * *

Indignant at not being invited to attend the funeral of an acquaintance, a man angrily told the bereaved: "Please God we shon 'ave a funeral in our family some day, then yo'll see w'o'll be asked."

* * *

"An' 'ow's yer 'usband?" a woman enquired of a friend she had not seen for a long time.

"Oh, e's jed a month cum next Toosday wik."

"Goo on. Wha' did 'e die on?"

"Oh, 'e just went to slape in 'is cheer, an' w'en 'e woke up 'e was jed."

* * *

Advertisement outside undertaker's yard: Funerals completely furnished. Large sized coffins £5. Small size coffins £3. Why not try one?

DEATH AND FUNERALS

The family breadwinner had been killed at work, and while he lay laid out upstairs in his home the employer called to console the widow. He discoursed at length on the many virtues of his late employee, speaking of his attention to work, his gentility and good temper. As he spoke the widow's amazement grew and grew. In the end she could contain herself no longer. "Goo upstairs, our Sarah," she whispered to her daughter, "an' 'ave another look, an' see if it really is yer faether."

DOMESTIC

The daughter of the house had returned from a spell in domestic service.

" 'Arriett's cum wum," explained the mother. " 'Er 'ad such a dale o' code baecon for breakfast, an' 'Arriett's one as cor stummack code baecon, an' the missus was a 'ard 'ooman. 'Er put on my girl summat crule. So 'Arriett cum back to 'er mother an' the missis did maek a bother at 'er gooin' off sudden like. But 'Arriett doe care for service. 'Er's sich a one for 'er pals, and some missises is against 'em 'avin' their pals perpetual."

*　　*　　*

A mother asked her small child what she was drawing.

"I'm drawing God."

"But you can't draw God, because nobody knows what He is like."

"They soon will . . . when I've finished this drawing."

*　　*　　*

A man called at the gasworks and said a chap named Jones had met him and asked him to say that there was a bad leak at the Jones's house.

"Whereabouts is the Jones's house?" he was asked.

"Oh," said the messenger, "I doe know weer the 'ouse is, but they'm left the kay next dore to it."

*　　*　　*

A Cradley Heath man had sent his small son in search of his lost fowl.

"Well, 'ave yer found 'em?" he enquired when the boy returned.

"Ah, I've put 'em in the pen."

"Weer wun um?"

"One was altogether, ten by theirselves, and three among one o' Newton's."

*　　*　　*

A small child, having been put to bed with the light turned down, called to her mother because she was frightened to be in the dark.

"You needn't be frightened," said the mother. "God is in the room with you, and you can't come to any harm."

"Well," said the child, "Grandmother's in bed in the next room, and she's got a candle. Let her have God and I'll have the candle."

DOMESTIC

Another child called downstairs: "Come and put the light on so that I can see to cough."

*　　*　　*

The new maid was dusting the pictures.

"Be careful with those pictures, Mary. Those are all old masters."

"Oh, missus," gasped the maid. "What a lot o' times yo' must a bin married."

*　　*　　*

"Yo' must think we'm med o' money," complained a man to his wife. "Yo've 'ad that electric fire burning' the 'ole o' this day."

"Doe yo' worry," she said triumphantly. "It ay our'n. I borrowed it from next dore."

*　　*　　*

The burglar had been surprised by the householder, who had him covered with an old army revolver.

"Yo' be careful wi' that thing, mister," said the burglar nervously.

The householder was equally nervous: "Doe be frit," he said, "it ay loaded."

*　　*　　*

"What's that you'm 'ommerin' down there?" shouted a wife to her husband in the cellar.

"I'm making' a 'andcart."

"What's the good adoin' that; yo' cor get it up the steps when you'm maed it?"

"Well, I con tekt it to pieces, cor't I?"

"How bin yer?"

"O, rubbin' an warin' like the ode boat."

The child was paying no attention to his mother's warnings about crossing the road.

"Well, goo on with yer, an' doe yo' blaeme me when you'm run over an' killed."

DOMESTIC

A housewife saw a rent collector heading up the path. She rapidly instructed her son to answer the door, then hid behind the curtain.

"W'eer's yer mother?"

" 'Er's out, mister."

"Oh! is 'er," said the collector glancing at the bottom of the curtain. " 'Ow long 'as 'er taken ter gooin' out without 'er feet?"

* * *

Sammie was small, not very bright, and known to be dominated by a masterful wife.

"Bin scrappin' with the missis lately, Sammie?" asked one of his pals when he arrived at the pit one morning.

"O, arr! 'Er wus in a awful temper this mornin'; a bit wuss than usual 'er was, 'er shied a sorcepon at me, an' I ony just got out o' the rode in time."

"And what did yo' dew?"

"Dew? Dew?" said Sammie hotly. "I dey auf slam the dore w'en I cum out."

* * *

A man who had built a small bungalow took a friend to see it.

" 'Ow dun yer like it?"

"I doe like the winders."

"They'm bay winders."

"Goo on! If they bay winders, what bin 'em?"

* * *

Conversation piece:

"I luvs every inch o' the ground as my wife walks on."

"Arr . . . an' I luvs every inch o' the ground as my wife's got cummin' to 'er."

* * *

A man trying to sweep his chimney, sent his little boy outside to see when the brush came out at the top. The lad kept running back to say there was no brush to be seen, so the man continued to add sections of rod and sent the brush higher. Still it failed to appear. Suddenly, the woman from the next house came running out.

What the 'ell dun yo' think you'm up to?" she screamed "Doe yo' forget my ode mon works on the night shift, and 'e's atryin' to get a bit o' slape, an' you'm shoved 'im out o' bed twice."

40

DOMESTIC

A Bilston housewife was heard cussin' and blindin' on the step of her house. Asked what was the matter she said: "It's the milkman, 'e's bin an' gone an' ay cum agen."

*   *   *

Nagged by his wife about his continual visits to the pub, a Black Country man could stand it no longer. He rounded on his wife, who was in full spate, and shouted: "If yo've got anythin' ter say, shut yer faerce!"

*   *   *

"I'm fed up wi' life," explained a man who was found by his wife suspended from a rafter by a rope round his middle.

"Yo' cor 'ang yerself like that," she said. "Why doe yer put it round yer neck?"

"Ah, I tried that," he grumbled. "An' I very nigh stranged meself."

"Bin a good settee, 'as this. It's stood some sittin' on."

"You've got nothin' to do; why doe you peint the mangle?" said a wife to her unemployed husband. "There's plenty o' peint in the attic. It woe tek yer long to dew."

Some time afterwards she heard a noise on the stairs.

"What am yer doin' on the stair, Joe," she called.

"Gettin' the mangle up to peint it like yo' said. The peint's up 'ere, ay it?"

*   *   *

Sent out by his wife to get a prop to hold up the clothes line, the husband returned with a long piece of wood which he fondly hoped would serve the purpose.

"What a fule yo' are," said his wife. "There's no nick in the top to 'old the line firm."

"Oh, that's all right; 'old it under the line while I get a pair of steps as 'ull reach, an' I'll soon saw a nick in it."

"What yo' want steps for ? Prop it against the 'ouse, and then yo' can reach it from the upstairs winder."

41

DOMESTIC

Two householders were discussing the merits of coal fires versus gas fires for the parlour.

"Best o' these gas fires," enthused one, "yo' doe 'ave to kip litin' 'em like yo' dew coal uns. Why we 'ad one put in our parlour three wiks agoo an' it ay gone out yet."

* * *

A housewife was behind with her payments for groceries.

"What do you do with your money," the shopkeeper complained.

"Yo' ay bin lucky in the draw lately else yo'd 'ave 'ad sum," the woman explained.

"I don't know what you mean, lucky in the draw. I want my money."

"Yo' be careful what yo' say," the woman cautioned. "If yo' doe watch out we shor put yer naeme in the 'at next wik when me mon 'as 'is wages."

> "Trouble wi' yo' . . . yo' con see through a brick wall yo' con, yo'm so clever. An' w'en yo've sane through it, yo'm lookin' at summat as ay theer."

A domestic drudge complained of her hard lot, and said she never had any enjoyment.

"But you enjoy going to sleep," said her mistress.

"How can I?" she replied. "The minit I lies down I'm asleep, an' the minit I wakes, I got to get up. When is there time to enjoy it?"

* * *

A woman was giving a dressing down to her three sons, who were in the habit of staying out till the small hours.

"Yo' three bin a tidy pair, if ever there was one. Las' night it were arf past fower this mornin' afore yo' comes in. An' if you'm goin' ter stop 'ere now, yo' can bugger off."

"Orl rite, missis," was the reply. "Weer we bin agen we can go afore–that's 'ow it is."

* * *

A group of children were discussing where babies came from. Said one little girl: "The milkman brung ours. I sid it on 'is cart. Families supplied."

42

DOMESTIC

A little chap was screaming 'murder' and neighbours came rushing in to see what was the matter.

"Doe get excited," his mother told them. "I'm only puttin' a clane shirt on 'im."

* * *

Wife yelling from the basement to her husband upstairs: "Cum down quick, the kitchen's flooded."

"What yer makin' a fuss about?" he shouted back. "Yo' bay a-drounded yet. Call up agen w'en yo' bin, an' I'll cum down."

* * *

A man was met by a friend hurrying down the street.

"Weer bist goin', Bill?"

"I'm goin' to the doctor's."

"What's the matter? Bin yer bad?"

"No, it's the missis. When I got wum I found 'er was a 'angin'."

"Strewth! 'Ave yer cut 'er down?"

"No, 'er wor jed."

* * *

"I daresay yo' think my 'usband give me this blued eye," said a housewife to a visitor. "Well 'e dey. I catched agen the cubbord. Not but what 'e used ter knock me about summat crule, but 'e gid over cos 'e sed it maede me look so ode."

* * *

A Bilston man started to learn French. He came home one night anxious to impress his wife, and ran in to her crying: "Araminta, je t' adore."

"Shut it yerself," she answered.

* * *

A small boy told his mother that while she had been out his little sister had been naughty.

"He's been naughty the best," cried his sister.

43

DOMESTIC

"Bist thee cummin' or bist thee baint?" shouted a mother to her young son playing in the street.

"Bist thee goin' to 'it me? If thee bist, I baint," the youngster yelled back.

"I wud ef I cud, but ef I cor' ow con I?"

A Gornal man called downstairs to his wife, who had never learned to tell the time: "Ria, what time is it?"

"The little finger's a 'angin' straight down, an' the big 'uns p'intin' to the pantry door."

* * *

"Bist never gooin' ter stop yer gab? I'm gettin' tired a lissnen to yo're blather."

"I ay got time ter stop, I gos ter bed at nine o'clock every night."

* * *

The servant girl was in trouble for having broken a window.

"What can yer expect when I'm always a-clanin' it?" she protested. "It's bound ter wear thin sum time."

* * *

"Me missis is alus botherin' me to clane me tathe, but never agen. The fust time I did it I cort a code an' I've 'ad it ever since."

* * *

Returning from an errand, a little girl said to her mother: "There ay auf some trouble at the Jones's. They've 'ad a card in the winder for wiks, 'Boy wanted,' an' now 'er's got a baby girl."

* * *

• A small child told not to play with matches or he might get his nice curly hair burnt off, enquired: "Is that why grandpa's bald?"

44

"Yor cote doe 'ang well," said a young man who rather fancied himself in his Sunday best to a companion. "Why doe yer try one o' these 'ere coat 'angers? I've got one."

Meeting the following Sunday afternoon, his friend remarked. "I've bought one o' them coat 'angers, but they doe auf mak yer shoulders ake."

"I bin 'as I bin, an' if I ay, I cor 'elp it."

A small boy returning home from school was told he had a new brother.

"Where did you get him from–the Co-op?"

"No, from the doctor's."

"Cor! Yo' see, w'en father comes 'ome there wo' auf be a row."

*　　*　　*

"What are you poking about with that stick under the door for?" said a collier who was waiting in the early morning to walk with a friend to the pit.

"Well, yo' see, me missus doe get up early, an' her likes the dore locked an' the kay pushed under it. I'm tryin' ter get the kay back, as I aye sure if I locked the dore."

*　　*　　*

Mother to small boy: "What dun yer want a fresh 'anky for? I only gid yer one last Sunday wik. 'Ave yer got a code or summat?"

*　　*　　*

From the bedroom of the twins came the mingled sounds of loud sobbing and hearty laughter.

"What's gooin'on up there, yo' tew?" shouted their mother.

"Nuthin'," chuckled one. "Ony yo' gid Johnny tew baths an' I dey 'ave nar'un."

*　　*　　*

The parents of a little girl given to swearing prevailed upon a constable to have a word with her. Meeting the child in the street, the policeman said he had heard that she was constantly using wicked words–and how naughty it was.

45

"And who told you?" she enquired.

"A little bird."

"Fancy that! An' I feed the little bugger every morning."

* * *

"Did yo're ode mon deliver 'is speech at the werk's dinner?"

" 'E must a' dun. 'E was speechless when 'e got whum."

* * *

"That was a very nice letter from Patrick offering you marriage, Mary. What shall I say in reply for you?"

"Tell 'im, mum, if yo' plaze, that when I get me wages raised nex' month, mum, I'll start ter save fer the weddin' things."

"If yode a bin me son, I'd 'ave 'ad yer drowned at birth."

A man went to Oldbury market to buy a pair of shoes. Returning after an absence of several hours, his wife asked for an explanation.

"Well," said he, "the string as ties 'em together ay very long as' yo' cor tek very big strides."

* * *

"I'm gooin' ter run over to me mother's for a minute. I'll be back in auf hour."

* * *

Lady hiring new maid: "We are all vegetarians and should expect you to become one. Have you any objection?"

Applicant: "Well, mum, it depends. Is beer a vegetable?"

* * *

Relating how a neighbour behaved when pinching her finger in the door: " 'Er screamed aloud under 'er breath."

* * *

· Housewife's lament: "I'll tell thee what it is; it takes more money for one thing and another than it does for anything else at our 'ouse."

FOOD

A maid describing her new place to a friend:

"I shore stay theer; yo' should see the tack as they buys for the kitchen. Why, my chap at the wagon werks grases the wales with better stuff than we'm expected to ate for butter."

* * *

A customer of the Co-op asked the assistant if he had got a hambone. The man found one from which nearly all the ham had been carved. "Here you are missis, you can have that for nothing."

"No I shor 'ave it for nothin'," she said indignantly. "No fear. I'm goin' ter pay. I ay that saft as to lose me divi on it."

* * *

Two workmen on their way home, pausing to watch the Rotomat go round in a new cafe.

"Eh, mate, what dun they do wi' all them chickens?"

"Why, they cuts 'em up an' sells the bits."

"Oh, ah! An' what's the dearest bit?"

"The back legs, yer fule."

* * *

Taking tea with a friend, a guest was very appreciative of the new bread that was on the table.

"We never gets new bread at our 'ouse," he said. "I ay auf enjoyed it. Saeve a bit o' that loaf till I cums agin."

* * *

A digestion sufferer had reached the stage when he imagined that almost everything he ate upset his stomach. He was consequently practically living on slops. When he returned home from work one evening, his wife produced his usual ration of bread and milk.

"Tek it away," he ordered, "an' goo out an' bring back a big pork pie, an' a large bottle o' stout."

"Are yer mad?" asked his wife. "Why it ull kill yer."

"Yo' do as I tells yer, an' fetch it," he commanded.

She did as he requested, and after he had eaten the pie and drank the stout, he sat back in his chair and began to smoke his pipe. Then he looked down at his stomach and said: "Now, let's settle it once an' for all. Who's goin' to be gaffer, yo' or me?"

FOOD

Two navvies about to start their mid-day meal.

" 'ow is it, Bert, you'm titenin' yer belt afore yo' starts to 'ave yer male? You'n got enoo, ay yer?"

"Well, the missis ay gid me quite so much fittle this mornin', but if yer titens yer belt afore yer starts, it maks yer think as yo've 'ad more than yo' 'ave."

*   *   *

"Faether, my egg's a bad 'un!"
"It tay a bad 'un, they'm all fresh laid."
"I'm sure it's a bad 'un, faether."
"I tell thee it tay. Get it down thee."
"Faether . . ."
"What now . . .?"
" 'Ave I got t'ate the bake and legs as well?"

*   *   *

A commercial traveller persuaded a small shop keeper to try a tin of a new kind of biscuit. Calling the following month, he asked how they had sold.

"I shor 'ave any more o' them sort," the shopkeeper told him. "Why, a tin o' the ode sort lasted a month, and your'n wun gone in a fortnit!"

"These 'ere eggs am boiled 'ard again, soft enough."

He ca auf ate," the carver was told when about to serve one of his guests to some beef. "Give 'im a piece as wo bend, Gaffer."

"Put another 'elpin' on 'is plaete," said another guest, pointing out his mate to the person carrying a sucking pig.

The carver looked across at the man indicated. "Joe, your mate says you can eat a sucking pig; is that so?"

"Ar!" he answered. "How big?"

FOOD

Boy watching his pal eat an apple: "Gie us a bit."

"Shor."

"Leave us the cor, then."

"There ay goin' to be no cor."

* * *

A boy was serving a lady in a small general shop. Said the lady: "Your hands are clean, but your arms are filthy, why didn't you wash your arms?"

"I 'aven't washed me 'onds; I've bin 'elpin' mother to clane the tripe."

* * *

"I think, cook, we must part this day month."

"Whatever for, mum? Yo' as yer own in almost everythin', an' there's never anythin' we 'as in the kitchen as is tasty but w'at I sends a bit up to the dinin' room."

* * *

At a cheap eating house it was customary on pancake day to fry for regular patrons as many pancakes as they could eat, free of charge.

A customer determined to make the most of the opportunity had already consumed a large number. "Just one more," he said, "Just one one, and then–?"

"And then what?" asked the proprietor anxiously.

"Bring me some thick 'uns."

* * *

Two miners entombed in a pit.

"Bist orlright, Bill?"

"I should be, Joe, if we'd got sum 'am to 'ave sum 'am an' eggs . . . if we'd got the eggs."

* * *

The morning after his first night in jail, a prisoner was brought his breakfast of 'skilly.'

"What's that?" he demanded.

"That's your breakfast," said the warden.

"Oh, that cor be fer me, I bain't bad. P'raps it's fer the mon next doer. I con ate some mate an' taters."

49

FOOD

A man whose wife was absent from home was doing his own house-keeping.

" 'Ere's a nice bit o' meat," said the butcher. "I kep' it for yer. It's as tender as a 'oman's 'eart."

"Oh! If that's it gie me a pound o' sausage."

*   *   *

"I had four kinds of cake at the party," said the girl when she returned home. "Plum cake, currant cake, seed cake and stomach ache."

*   *   *

The sick man had been on a diet, but now that the doctor could see no hope of his recovery, he told the man's wife to let him have whatever he fancied to eat.

"The doctor says yo' can 'ave what yo' like to ate, Joe," she called up the stairs. "What dun yer fancy?"

"I fancy sum o' that 'am what's a 'angin' up in the kitchen," he shouted down weakly.

"Oh, yo' cor 'ave none o' that," she said. "We'm a saervin' it fer the funeral."

*   *   *

A woman was talking to the vicar about his sermon. "I doe un'ner-stand that 'ere remark o' your'n, constant drippin' ull wear away a stone. I've bin 'avin' it for breakfast an' tay for fower months an' I've put a stone on."

*   *   *

"Ah, I knows them sort as put on so much side. I lived with one as a cook once," reminisced a Gornal woman.

"When they wanted chicken soup for dinner, they used to bring me a skinny chicken and tode me to 'ang it over a sorcepan o' code water, lat it simmer for a bit an' serve it with pepper an' vinegar, an' then they ate it with a fork."

*   *   *

"I doe think much o' this tripe, it's stringy," said one woman to another in a seaside restaurant.

• "Well," said her companion. "If I was yo' ide tek me veil off afore I 'ad any more. It'll taeste better."

50

FOOD

A woman complained to her cook that a chicken served at table had one leg missing. To excuse herself, the cook invited her mistress to the fowlpen to see for herself that every bird in the pen had only one leg. The woman duly followed her, and sure enough, the time being evening, such did seem to be the case. However, the woman made a 'shooing' noise, and immediately each bird flustered and revealed a second leg.

"Ah," said the cook quickly. "That's all right, but yo' dey shoo the one on the table."

* * *

A small boy taken out to tea stretched his hand over the table to reach for the jam. " 'Aven't yer got a tongue?" asked his mother.

"Ar," he said quickly, "but it ay long enough."

* * *

" 'Ave yer brought 'am for breakfast?" asked one workman of another.

"Don't ask me if I've brought 'am for me breakfast," was the gloomy reply. "I 'ear enough about 'am at 'ome in a mornin' afore I cum. I'm sick o' the name o' 'am. Am yer goin' ter get up? Am yer goin' to goo ter werk this mornin'? Am yer tryin' ter lose yer job? Am this, am t'other? My missis torks o' nuthin' but 'am from six o'clock in the mornin' till I gets out o' the 'ouse."

* * *

"If we wun be'hind before, ween finished fust," said a man sitting with a friend at the works dinner.

* * *

A Black Country man who posed as a medium at Sunday evening seances, went under control, then suddenly astonished the circle by saying: "Ode tight, I'm comin' out now, I waent me supper. I only 'ad a bit o' bread an' cheese for me dinner, an' no tay."

* * *

Visitor taking tea with a friend: "Ave yer got mice 'ere? It sounds just like as if they'm scratchin' the other side the wall."

"Oh, no, they'm 'avin' celery with their tay next dore—we con allus tell."

FOOD

Man on a slop diet describing his feelings when his family were taking their meal of 'mate an' taters' as–"Like bein' muzzled in a cook shop."

*   *   *

A workman, after a big feed and plenty of beer provided by the proprietor at a works dinner, was called upon to propose a vote of thanks. Having imbibed freely and finding himself unable to get to his feet, he said: "I ain't got nothin' to say, but I must say it sittin' down as I cor stand up."

THE
GARRULOUS
CHAINMAKER

"These ere doctors, if yo' ay feelin' up to the mark an' yo' goo to ask 'em wot's the matter, the very fust question they askin' yer is ow much beer dun yer drink. Well, I doe 'ave a lot considerin' the waerk I does. Wen yo'm makin' big kaebles, yo' 'as to 'ave sum beer, else yo'd drap jed. Yo'm swettin' most on it out on yer.

"I've on'y bin on the Staet onst, an' wen I was took bad I went to see ode Doctor Tibbetts at Craedley. A good ode sort, 'e wun; 'e day trate yer like a panneler at nine an' a tanner a piece or watever they gettin' a 'ear to attend to the likes o' we. 'E says, 'Jim, yo'll 'ave to knock off the beer,' almost afore I'd said a waerd—well, 'e'd put me on the box an' after a time I 'ad a notice to appear at Dudley to be specially examined afore one o' these 'ere Government doctors. I suppose they thoughtin' I was a-shammin'. Wen I got the notice I went to the ode doctor's surgery to ask 'im wot I was to say was the matter wi' me. The ode mon 'adn't tode me up to then.

"Another thing, I says, 'Doctor, if yo' knowin' wot's the matter wi' me, why shud I go b— ing off to Dudley?' When 'e tode me it was the law, I says, if it's the law, I supposin' I must goo. 'Well,' says 'e, 'yo'm run down a bit.' I think 'e said it was nervous ability, or summat 'o that; so I gos up afore this 'ere bloke at Dudley, an' after 'e'd tapped me on me legs an' maede me nearve jump, 'e taps me chest an' ceterer, and says 'Put yer clothes on agen', an' wen I was a-doin' it, 'e says, all sudden like, ' 'Ow much beer dun yer drink?'

"O' course, 'e couldn't let the subjec' aloon, ony moor than me own mon could. So I tode 'im as we chaps as maede chain 'ad to 'ave a drap. 'E says, ' 'Ow much, an' wot sort is it?' I says, 'Malt an' 'ops mostly, wot we maeks at wum–as for the noo-fangled kemical stuff as they sellen at the pubs, I on'y 'as four or five quaerts ony day, as too much o' that muck, I reckon, doe do anybody ony good.'

"I says, 'Why, for the fouerpenny o' my young days yo've got to pay eightpunce now, an' not near as strong. The beer in them days was that thick it was fude an' drink.' I tode 'im we used to get a ode sammon tin, put a bit o' wire for a 'ondle, an' 'ad it filled for a penny.

" 'Well, doe 'ave any more for a bit,' says the doctor chap.

"I dey tell 'im, but I ay gooin' to stop 'avin' me beer to please 'im, nor onybody else, no blinkin' fear.

"Ar, we chaienmaekers 'ad a goodish drap o' drink in the ode days, an' wen we'd got the money, we dey stick to beer, neither. We allus went into the pub afore we started waerk an' 'ad a drap o' rum so as to get gooin.' Many's the time I bin in that pub at six o'clock in the mornin' an' adn't left it till 11 o'clock the night afore. Well, they doe let 'um kape the publics open them number o' 'ours now, an' a dam'd good job, tew.

"Afore I cum off the box was quite a month, the ode Doctor Tibbetts, he says, 'ave to go slow on the drink, as you've 'ad 'igh blood pressure, as well as the naervous ability.'

"It doe matter wot's the matter wi' yer, 'Yo must knock off yer beer.' That's the on'y thing these 'ere doctors con think on to say. Just like b— parrots, they bin. We cor dew our job on code tay. When I was a kid we 'ad it for we breakfusses, an' if they doctors swetted at their waerk like we dun, they'd waent beer theyreselves, an' a lot on it. Ony rode, I shon 'ave a drap as long as I've got ony money to buy it. So let's goo an' 'ave a quaert. But these ay like the good ode days, yo' cor get drunk now on beer, an' the wiskey's tew dear.

"Torkin' o' the ode days–One Crismus, forty 'ears agoo it 'ud be, I cum across me bruther Ali in a pub near 'is 'ouse an' we started 'avin' tews o' wiskey, tew penniwuth a-piece, 'ach time, an' the ode sargent cum in an' I says, 'Wot un yer 'ave, sargent?' 'E says 'I'll 'ave a quartern wi' yo',' an' as we 'ad tews 'e 'ad quarterns. The ode sargent went fust, an' wen I cum to get on my faete I wor tew stiddy, an' wen I started to goo up the 'ill tew our ouse, as I climbed up I fun I was

54

acomin' back. Well, I says, I'll goo to me bruther's close by, but I see the sargent a-watchin' out, so I tried to dodge 'im be'ind a piller, but 'e sid me. The sargent says, 'It's no good, Joe, yo'm drunk,' he says, 'You'll 'ear about this,' an' 'e'd bin 'avin' quarterns at our expense, an' I tode 'im soo. Next day there cum a nock at the door, and I says 'W'ose that, misses?' an' 'er says, 'It's the sargent, ' 'e waents yo,' and he cums in an' 'onds me a bit o' paeper an' 'e says this ay at your'n expense ony rode up. It was a summons alrite. 'If yer cor appear, Joe,' 'e says, 'yo'd better send a quid an' yo'll get no chaenge out o' that.'

"I says, 'I got ter goo ter waerk, we'm busy, an' O ay got a quid.' I sends the missis to the boss at 'is wum in the evenin' an' tode 'er to be sure an' see 'im an' tell 'im I 'adn't got a quid, an' I expected I should 'ave to goo down the rale. I noo as we was busy an' caeble-makers wun short. The boss's missis dey waent ourn to see the gaffer, 'er says 'Let 'im goo to prison, serve 'im rite,' but 'e cum out an' 'eard all about it, and 'e says 'e wo lave off waerk if it cosses twenty quid, so that wun alrite. Well, we wun gettin good money an' wiskey wor dear, an' the sargent 'e 'ad me about a month after that, an' I 'ad to pay agen. Once a fortnit 'e 'ad me bruther an' then me. Then 'e gid us a rest for a bit.

"Well, we cor all be tachers an' parsons, sum on us must maeke a bit o' caeble chaien sumtimes."

LOVE AND MARRIAGE

"Wilt thou," intoned the clergyman, "have this woman to be thy wedded wife . . . . ?"

"Ah, I s'pose I've got to now. But I'd sooner 'ave 'ad 'er sister, Sal."

"And succour her and sustain her?"

"Ah . . . I'll feed 'er on mutton chops, an' ale, and put a bit o' flesh on 'er boons."

* * *

"Somebody said yo' was gooin' to get married to one of them Jones chaps," said a girl to her friend. "Which un is it?"

"Oh, it's the one with a waetch."

* * *

"Yo'm a little duck, ain't yer?" said a young man to a girl he had grown tired of, as they walked along the cut side.

"Ah," the girl sighed blissfully. As she nestled up to him he pushed her into the water. "Well," he said, " 'ere's a chance to 'ave a swim, then."

* * *

"Sholl I ode yer 'ond, darlin'?"

"S'all rite, luv. It ay 'eavy."

* * *

A man who had been married previously invited a friend to come and meet his new wife.

" 'Er ay much to look at," was the friend's whispered comment when he saw her. "Why, 'er's got no taeth an' 'er nose is broke, an' 'er wears glasses."

"Well, yo' needn't shisper, 'er's deaf as well. But 'er's got a good heart, and w'ats more 'er's a damned good cook." said the proud husband.

* * *

A Gornal man's first experience of 'walking out' with a girl.

"I dey know wat to say at fust, as I'd never dun no cortin afore, so I axed 'er if 'er waented goin' with, an' 'er sed as 'er dey mind, so I put me arm round 'er waest, an' then it was all right."

LOVE AND MARRIAGE

"Missis, yo'er ode mon's a bit of a 'ot 'un, ay 'e? I doe think 'e'd waet long afore 'e'd 'ave another if anythin' 'appened to yo'."

"Well . . . all I can say is, whoever 'er is, I doe wish 'er any 'arm, but God 'elp 'er!"

*   *   *

Ideal helpmate:

> "I likes a wife wi' a good strong arm
> An' at mornens at werk 'er goes a-dustin';
> 'Er'll kape the pantry full if 'er ony wull
> Goo out fower days a-washin'."

*   *   *

"Spakin' o' women," said a man to his friend, "they never knows wot they doo waent, an' w'en they'm got it they doe waent it. There's always somethin' wrong, accordin' to 'em, an' they ay satisfied till yo've put it right, an' w'en yo've put it right, it's flamin' wrong."

*   *   *

Commented a young husband to his mate: "My wife's an angel."

"Yo' always did 'ave all the luck," grumbled the other.

"Mine ay even jed."

*   *   *

A foreigner attending a golden wedding reception, asked what it meant.

The host put his arm lovingly round his wife's waist. "It means that we have lived together for 50 years," he explained.

"And now," said the foreigner, "I suppose you are going to marry her?"

*   *   *

A man with a nagging wife was out shopping with her one day when he saw a notice in a dentist's window: "Teeth stopped on moderate terms."

Turning to her thoughtfully, he said... "I wonder what 'e'd tek ter stop yer gab?"

LOVE AND MARRIAGE

"Ow dun yer like bein' married, Sairey?"

"Oh, I think it's luvly, an' wouldn't chaenge back again for anythin'. The only drawback is I doe care for me 'usband much, but there, yo' cor 'ave everythin'."

* * *

"W'at dun yer dew w'en yer waents to get rid o' yer missus, Joe? I'm damned sick o' mine. Cort yet get a divorce or summat? I've 'eard as yo' con get one if yer can prove as yer wife's flat-footed."

"Doe tork like a fule, that' ony w'en the foot's in another mon's flat."

* * *

"I'm off to Brummagem to buy a truss o' hay," a young man told his friend.

"What do you want that for? Yo' doe kape a pony."

"No, yer fule, I'm goin' to get married, an' all the women want's summat to get married in."

* * *

A woman was told that another woman who had recently lost her husband had got married a second time.

"Any 'ooman as marries again," she said with feeling, "dey deserve to lose 'er fust mon."

* * *

A man who was always chewin' went into a jeweller's shop to buy a wedding ring.

"Eighteen carat?" queried the jeweller.

" 'Course I bay . . . I'm chewin' bacca."

* * *

"I've bin gooin' out with yer for a wik, an' I doe even know yer Christian naeme. W'at is it?"

"Why 'Arold, o' course; I thought as yo' noo."

" 'Ow did yer get that silly naeme?"

"Don't yer know? It was took from the hymn ' 'Ark the 'Arold Angels Sing,' cos I was born on a Christmas Day."

" 'E doe know waet 'e does waent, but 'e waents it so badly, 'e'll 'ave a fit if 'e doe get it."

LOVE AND MARRIAGE

" 'Ow's yer wife, Bill?"

"Oh, 'er's all right till 'er gets summat else. But theer, I almost think 'er's 'ad everythin' now!"

*   *   *

"I'm walkin' out with a real toff now," a girl told her friend. "He doe bloe 'is tay with 'is mouth like we dun, 'e fans it with 'is 'at like a gen'lman."

*   *   *

A collier who had started courting, was advised that he would look much smarter if he took to wearing a 'dickey', which could be washed when necessary.

He adopted the suggestion, but meeting his friend a short time afterwards, he said, "I got one o' them 'dickeys' what yo' tode me about, but it ay near as warm as a shirt."

*   *   *

Walking in the country, the courting couple saw a cow and calf rubbing noses in the accepted bovine manner.

"Yo' know, me wench, seein' that meks me waent ter dew the saeme."

"Well goo on then affore they runs away."

*   *   *

"Was yo're missus tired after the party last night?"

" 'Er wor auf. 'Er cud 'ardly keep 'er mouth open."

*   *   *

"Darlin' . . . do you think it's true that all the world loves a lover?"

"No, I doe. Not since I called ter see yer faether."

59

"Who's that?" enquired a woman, entering a neighbour's house just as a man was coming out.

"That's our doctor," she was told. " 'E's bin ter see the babby about 'is rash."

"What, 'im a doctor? Why, if I'd a bit o' chalk I could draw a better doctor than 'im on the wall."

*   *   *

A man who had been injured in a motor accident was taken into the nearest public house.

"What's the matter?" he asked, becoming conscious.

"Yo'll be all rite, keep nice an' quiet," said one of the men who had carried him indoors. "We've just brought you to."

"Well, if yo' an'," replied the victim, "I doe remember. Bring me tew more."

*   *   *

"What's up wi' yo'?" said an old man to a young work-mate.

"I got a bile on me neck, an' it doe auf 'urt."

"Yah, yo' 'shud tek yer medicin' regular, like I do–five quaerts a day, an' I never 'ad a squilt let alone a bile all me life."

"Allo, Joe, yo've bin on the box, aye yer? 'Ave yer recuvered from the medsin as the doctor gid yer yet?"

Told by a doctor to open his mouth and put out his tongue, a boy stared first at the doctor, then at his mother.

"Doctor," said the mother, "the kid doe understand yo'er sort o' tork. Cum 'ere, Billie. Open yer gob an' put ye larrikin out."

*   *   *

A man complained of a sore toe which he thought was caused by a bad corn. He was advised to go to a chiropodist, which he did. On his return he was asked if the chiropodist did him any good.

"Oh, ah, it's better now; it was only me collar stud as 'ad slipped into me shoe."

MEDICAL

"Where do you feel this pain you complain of?" the doctor asked his extremely small patient.

"I doe rightly know," the man told him. "I'm that short, I cor tell whether it's me 'ead achin' or me corns a-botherin' me."

*   *   *

Reprimanded by her mistress for running upstairs after the doctor had told her she had a weak heart, the maid started to come down again.

"Whatever are you coming down for?"

"So's I con walk up like the doctor said."

*   *   *

A woman was describing a faith healing meeting.

"A mon walked into the 'all so lame 'e 'ad to use crutches. 'E was invited on to the platform an' we all prayed and 'e prayed and we prayed, and we prayed agen, an' at last 'e threw away one of 'is crutches, an' then we all prayed agen, 'arder than ever, an' throwin' away 'is remainin' crutch, 'e shouted–'I'm cured, I'm cured.' Then 'e fell off the platform an' broke 'is bloody neck."

*   *   *

Two men, having had a surgical operation, were in adjacent beds in the ward of a hospital.

"I don't feel so grand this morning," said one. "I think the doctor must have left his forceps inside me or summat."

"Ah!" said the other. "I'm feelin' a bit funny meself. Ah remember now, as I was a comin' round after they'd stitched me up, I 'eard one of them doctors say 'where's me 'at?' It makes yer think, doe it?"

*   *   *

A visitor seeing the inmate of a mental home wheeling a barrow upside down, went up to him and enquired gently why he didn't wheel it the right way up."

"If I did that," said the patient, "somebody might put somethin in it."

"Who the 'ell ud 'ave the stummick ake at that price?" said a man who was told by a pal "I 'ad brandy an' port mixed to ease the pain."

Black Country recipe for a cold:
Two penn' orth o' God 'elp me.
One dose o' ferther on.

The doctor was making out a record card for a woman patient.

"Name?"

"Brown."

"With an 'e'?"

"No, I've cum by meself. I've bin a widder two 'ear."

*　　*　　*

A child had been sent by her mother to enquire as to a neighbour's health. "I suppose," said the mother, "she thinks she's very ill, like she did yesterday."

"Well today," said the little girl, " 'er thinks 'er's jed."

*　　*　　*

A doctor, having done everything he could for a patient, informed the wife that it was useless to send for him again as her husband could not possibly survive for more than a few days. Nevertheless, in the middle of the night she sent for him again. He was furious at what he regarded as a fruitless journey: "What was the use after what I told you," he said, "fetching me out in the middle of the night to a dead man?"

"But I aye jed, doctor," came the patient's voice from the bedroom.

Anxious to placate the doctor, the wife shouted: "If the doctor says you're jed, yo' bin jed, so shut up, because 'e knows better than yo'."

*　　*　　*

Calling to see his patient, the doctor found that the man had died during the night. Somewhat puzzled, he asked the wife if she had carried out instructions and given the prescribed diet.

MEDICAL

"Yes," said the woman. "I followed instructions, 'cept I thought champagne and oysters a bit dear, so I gid 'im ginger beer an' welks; I dey think it 'ud mak ony difference."

* * *

A man who had had his hand injured asked the doctor if he would ever be able to play the piano.

"Oh, yes, as time goes on," the doctor assured him, "you'll be able to play the piano all right."

"That's strange," said the man, "becos I couldn't play it afore."

* * *

Two inmates of a mental home compared notes and decided that they were sane. They succeeded in obtaining an interview to discuss their release. As they approached the official's office, the one said to the other, "I'd better test yo' afore we goo in, as I ay so sure as I was. Now yo' tell me . . . what am I holdin' in my hands behind my back?"

"A blinkin" motor lorry," was the prompt reply.

His fellow inmate looked disgusted. "Cheat," he said. "Yo' saw me pick it up."

"I ay ser bad. But I aye as well as what I was affower I wuz as bad as I am now."

" 'Ow bin yer, Joe, yo' doe look tew good."

"O, I'm orlrite, but when I'm aloookin' at onythin' a lot, a little spot cums in front o' me eyes."

"Yo' waent's to goo to that doctor bloke at the clinic, 'e'll soon put yer eyes right."

The pair met again some time afterwards:

"Bin yo'er sight only better?"

"O, ah! I went to the doctor like yo' said an 'e gid me sum glasses. It's wonderful what they'm dun fer me, an' all. Them spots am three times the size they was afore."

63

MEDICAL

Patient advised to go to the seaside to convalescence:

"I doe waent ter goo to the sayside. If I waents to look at waeter I con 'ave a walk along the cut."

"Me mon's bin took bad, but there's nuthin' the matter with im, an' nobody knows what it is."

It was a case of triplets, and in due course the father was taken to see them. He looked earnestly at each babe in turn, then pointed to the middle one.

"Doctor," he said " I think I'll kip that 'un."

MISCELLANEOUS

"Yo' think yo'm clever, doe yer missus? But I cud gie yer a wrinkle or tew."

"Arr, Florrie . . . an' by the look o' yo're faece yo' wo' miss 'em neither."

* * *

Told by a bank clerk that it was impossible to cash a crossed cheque over the counter, the obliging young lady said: "I don't mind coming round your side of the counter, if you have no objection."

* * *

Conjuror: "For my next trick, will any member of the audience give me an egg?"

Voice from the gods: "If any on us 'ad got one, mate, yode 'ave 'ad it long agoo."

* * *

Conversation over dropped handkerchief, retrieved by lads at village dance:

"Is this 'ersens?"

"No, it's shesens."

* * *

The lecturer was stressing how people resort to the use of vegetable metaphors when describing a woman. "Her cheeks are **roses,** her lips **cherry,** her hands **lily,** her mouth **rosebud;** complexion like a **peach,** and her breath as fragrant as **honeysuckle.**"

"Yo'n fergot one, ony road," shouted a listener, when he had finished.

"What's that?"

" 'Er tongue–it's a bloody scarlet-runner."

"I am as I am, an' I cor be ony ammerer no matter 'ow I am."

"Two dozen boxes o' matches?" said the shopkeeper, "Why, missis, yo' 'ad a dozen ony the other day."

"Arr, I've used them up. It's me ode man. Y'see 'e's deaf an' dumb an' talks in 'is sleep."

65

MISCELLANEOUS

Said a miser who had just been pulled out of the canal: "You may have saved my life, young man. I would give you ten shillings, but I only have a pound note."

"That's easy put right," said his rescuer. "Just jump in again."

* * *

"Shall I mind the shop while you goes out?" asked a small boy, bursting suddenly into a grocery store.

"But I'm not going out," said the grocer.

"Oh, yes yo' are, 'cos yer wife's fell in the cut."

* * *

Kindly lady to street beggar: "Tell me, my poor man, is your blindness permanent?"

"Looks like it, missis. Times is so bad I cor see no chance o' retirin'."

* * *

Asked to buy a raffle ticket for a pageant, a Darlaston man said he wouldn't know what to do with a pageant if he won it.

* * *

"Peers or people is the vital issue of the day," said an enthusiastic canvasser for votes at one of the Dudley election campaigns.

"Well," said the canvassed one, "if yo' puts it that way, I'm for the piers, cos Blackpool's got three, an' Dudley ay got a single one."

* * *

The 'draw' has been made and one fellow was staring disgustedly at his useless raffle ticket. His mate touched him on the shoulder: "It ay no use. You'm like the bloke what fell out o' the balloon—you bay in it!"

* * *

Said one pensioner to another: "Yo' know that sate just inside the park gaetes as yo' an' me was a-sittin' on yesterday? Well, I sot on it this mornin', an' it wor theer, an' I dey auf know about it when I cum tew."

66

MISCELLANEOUS

"The next dance will be a snake dance," announced the M.C. to dancers in a crowded ballroom.

"Snake dance?" shouted somebody. "What's a snake dance?"

Nobody knew what it was, so the M.C. explained. "The man on the door has only taken a few shillings, so not above half of you have paid. The snake dance comes to this: Those of you who 'snaked' in without paying can 'snake' out again."

* * *

"Everythin' I've planted ay 'ad a drop o' rain, an' w'at it 'as 'ad ay dun it ony good."

* * *

"Sorry, madam," said the cashier to the lady customer "Your account is overdrawn and my instructions are not to let you have any more money until the account is in credit."

"Oh, that's all right. If you'll say how much I owe you. I'll write you a cheque at once."

* * *

"What bin yer goin' ter do wi' all that 'ere dirt out of yer celery trench, Bill?" a gardener was asked.

"I'm goin' ter dig a 'ole up the garden to put it in, bay I, yer fule," he was told.

* * *

After a long soliloquy, the actor finally made his exit from the stage. Commented a voice from the Gods: " 'E's gone ter mek waeter."

* * *

Two young men were bathing from an old canal boat. Shouted the one in the boat to the one in the water: "Cum out an' get dressed. This boat's a-leakin'."

"Ah bay. I'm gooin' to dive in an stay down as long as I con; it's a-rainin' up 'ere."

* * *

It was pouring with rain. "Dun yer know what I thinks?" said one man to another, "I think's its gooen' ter clear up an' be wet."

67

MISCELLANEOUS

"What are the easiest weeds to kill?" a gardener was asked.

"Widow's weeds," chuckled the gardener. "Yo'm ony got ter say wilt thou? and they soon wilt."

* * *

A schoolgirl took her small brother into the sea to bathe. After a while the mother, who could only distinguish the head and shoulders of the girl above the water, called out: "Where's John?"

"It's orlright, mother," the girl shouted back. "I'm 'odin' 'is 'ond!"

* * *

As the farmer said: "At this time of 'ear an 'our's raen does mo'er good in five minutes than a month's would in a wik at any other time."

* * *

A man who had had a ticket in a raffle called at the shop kept by a woman who had promoted it, to hear how he had got on. The woman consulted a list of names. "Well, yo' am a lucky mon," she said. "If yo'd 'ad number 38 instead of number 39, yo'd a won a 20-stone baecon pig. As it is, yo've won a half pound jar o' drippin'."

* * *

Magistrate to defendant: "You are discharged with a caution. But remember, if you come here again you'll get twice as much."

* * *

A confirmed loafer who had been on Public Assistance for months and months, complained to a friend that payment was to be stopped.

When the friend pointed out that he couldn't really complain, considering the length of time he had been in receipt of public relief, he said: "It's all very well for yo' to talk like that, but doe yo' forget, thae'n 'ad the best 'ears of my life."

* * *

Conversation in the ruins of Dudley Castle:

"They dun say as 'ow sum o' these 'ere castles am 2,000 'ears ode."

* "Doe tork so saft, it's ony nineteen sixty-eight now. You'm overdoin' it a bit ay yer?"

68

MISCELLANEOUS

Friend to workmate who had just taken to wearing glasses: "Dost think they'm any good? Why, thee cosn't see as well now as thee coost, cost?"

*　　*　　*

The widow of a former Earl of Dudley was unveiling a statue erected to his memory.

"Who's 'er?" said one woman in the crowd to another.

"Which 'un?"

" 'Er what's makin' the spaich."

"Doe yo' know? 'Er's the monument's wife."

*　　*　　*

"What's R.I. mane, wot yo' sometimes see after the Queen's naeme?"

"Rial 'Ighness, yer fule."

*　　*　　*

A lady standing outside a bookseller's shop, stopped a policeman.

"Would you mind going into that shop and getting the latest catalogue?"

"Why not go in and get one yourself, madam?" the policeman asked, not unreasonably.

"Oh, I would," she replied, "but the circular I had said send a P.C. for list of books."

*　　*　　*

"How about money?" was the question put to Peter at the gate by a would-be angel.

"Every penny is equal to a million pounds here," said Peter.

"And what about time?"

"Every minute is a million years."

"Well," said the applicant, "lend me a penny"

"All right," said Peter, "in a minute."

*　　*　　*

Comment by a girl whose friend had failed to turn up at the time arranged: "Her woe cum now sure to."

69

A gardener, shopping in Darlaston, saw some special netting he thought suitable for his peas. "Is it good stuff?" he enquired.

"Of course," said the assistant. "In fact, it's rot proof."

"Ah, yes," said the gardener. "Rot proof it might be, but is it saef against mice?"

* * *

"Did Edison make the first loud speaker?"

"No, God! But Edison made the first one you could shut off."

* * *

A grocer's boy, trying to push a loaded handcart up a steep hill, was assisted by a passerby.

"Why don't yer boss send somebody with yer ter 'elp yer push?" asked the man.

"Well, 'e 'as talked about it," the boy explained. "But there, 'e says . . yo'll alus come across some bloody fool as ull 'elp yer on a 'ill."

* * *

A miserly farmer had the misfortune to fall down a well. His shouts brought his wife to the scene. She took one look and told him she would fetch a couple of farm hands to haul him to the surface.

"Hold on," he shouted. "What time is it?"

"Half past twelve."

"Oh, well. It only wants half an hour till dinner time. I can manage to swim about till then."

* * *

"I shor live long when I gets in the workus," said one ageing lady to another. "Two 'oomen from my strate went, an' they was so cruel to 'em it killed 'em. Dun yo' know, they put 'em in a bath."

"That chap on t'other side 'o the rode is the biggest thafe I ever cum across. If theer's nuthin' else about e'd stale the wind out o' yer bike tyres."

MISCELLANEOUS

Cross-examining solicitor to the victim in an assault case: "The last witness said the defendant struck you on the right side and you say on the left side."

"Well, p'raps 'e dey notice, but the chap as struck me is left 'onded."

*   *   *

"The happiest hours of my life," remarked the host wittily, "were spent in the arms of another man's wife–my mother."

A few evenings later, a friend of the host, attended a public dinner accompanied by his wife, attempted to lighten the proceedings by quoting the same 'bon mot'.

"The happiest moments of my life," he began, "were spent in the arms of another man's wife . . ." He gave an embarrassed pause, then burst out: "But I'm hanged if I can remember who the lady was."

*   *   *

Two men were arguing as to what it meant when one heard the cuckoo for the first time before anyone else. One said it meant good luck for the rest of the year, and the other that it meant something else, and so on. They finally appealed to a fellow workman for his view on the matter.

"It means yo' ay deaf," he answered promptly.

*   *   *

A Lye man was ploughing on a Sunday. Asked why he wanted to work on a Sunday, he replied: "Oh, I ay workin'. I'm ony gettin' it ready for the wate to be planted."

*   *   *

A customer in an outfitter's shop was trying on waistcoats. The first one went round him nearly twice. The price was four and sixpence (c. 1935). The next one he tried fitted him to a nicety.

"An' 'ow much is that un?" he asked.

"Same price as the other," said the assistant.

"Why, that's ridic'lus," said the man. "Why, it ay above auf the size, an' yo' waent four and six for it? Wrap the big un up. Yo' ay 'aving me like that."

71

MISCELLANEOUS

"I want a cake o' soap, please, missis."

"Do you want it scented?"

"No, I'll tek it with me."

* * *

"Don't yer see there's no road across 'ere?" roared a farmer at a group of workmen who were taking a short cut across his land.

"No," agreed one. "there doe seem ter be much of a rode, but ween put up wi' it."

* * *

A conjuror mysteriously producing eggs at a concert, said to a simple-looking lad on the front row. "Your mother can't get eggs laid without hens, can she?"

"Ar, she con," said the lad.

"Oh . . . how's that?"

" 'Er kapes ducks."

* * *

A woman was charged at the Police Court for assaulting a neighbour in biting a piece off her ear.

"Bound over to keep the peace for six months," said the magistrate.

"Sorry," said the offender. "But I gid it the cat."

* * *

A 20-stone innkeeper employed a potman who was so thin that customers jokingly nicknamed him Fat Jack. One day Fat Jack ran to his employer and called out: "I say, gaffer, yo' oughter cum and see the bloke what's just come in. Yo' call me thin. 'E's as thin as yo' and me put tergether."

* * *

The Mayor moved in Council that the park pool should be provided with a gondola, whereupon a business-like Councillor begged to move an amendment that instead of one gondola they should have a pair "so as they could breed."

Eventually becoming Mayor himself, the same gentleman was seen trying out the knives at the Town Hall banquet.

'"Mr. Mayor," said the waiter. "I think you will find the knives are quite sharp."

72

"Yes, I know," replied his Worship. "I cut my mouth last time."

It is said that the same Councillor advocated the covering over of the park pool to keep the ducks dry when it rained.

*   *   *

"Our party has got all the brains," said a political speaker.

"Ah," shouted a listener. "It's a pity they'm addled."

*   *   *

Said a man to a friend who lived in a neighbouring borough: "We'm just bought our Mayor a noo chein to put round 'is neck."

"Oh, we ay got a chein for ourn; we let's the beggar run loose," commented the other.

" 'E's so full o' lies as if 'e opens 'is mouth to spake there's sure to be one drap out."

A member of a Black Country council complained at a meeting that for the second Sunday morning in succession the water had been cut off.

"Good for the beer trade, Bill," remarked a fellow councillor, philosophically.

"Ah," said the complainant, "but yo' cor bile taters in beer."

*   *   *

Solicitor at inquest: "Was the car on your right side or your left?"

"I couldn't say. I'm a stranger to these parts."

*   *   *

The post-office official was known to be off-hand and haughty. "Will this letter get to London tomorrow if it's posted now?" he was asked.

"Certainly, it will."

"Well, it wo' then, cos it's addressed to Sheffield."

MISCELLANEOUS

A chainmaker noted for his bad language slipped on a banana skin and merely said "damn."

Commented an acquaintance: "Thee cossent cuss like thee cudst cuss, cost?"

*   *   *

Because there was a main road at the bottom, two boys were told to stop running down a steep hill.

"We ay runnin'," said one. "The rode's pushin' we."

"If yo' never cum back, it ull be tew soon fer me, an' I waern't ter tell yer even if I noo yo' was spakin' the truth I shouldn't belave yer."

A Gornal youth was carrying two cans of milk from the cowhouse to the dairy, slopping milk at every step. Told about it, he said: "Well, the more it slops, the less I shall 'ave ter carry, shor I?"

PECULIAR EXPRESSIONS

"A kitchen ile paintin'." (A side of bacon hung from a rafter.)

"A odin' down pin." (A tot of brandy.)

"Blow me bags out. (Having a good feed.)

" 'Er'd be better if 'er 'ad the knittin' board on a bit oftener." (Indicating a woman not overfond of work.)

"A tidy bit o' money tied to her frock." (Well to do.)

"I'm dummucked up." (Tired out.)

"Chate the grave." (Anyone who recovers after being given up by the doctors.)

"Lummickin looby." (A clumsy person.)

"A thumb bit." (Small portion of food held in the hand.)

Gems from Letters to the Pensions Department

Please send my money at once, as I have fallen in errors with the landlord.

* * *

In accordance with your instructions, I have given birth to twins in the enclosed envelope.

* * *

You have changed my little girl to a boy, does that make any difference?

* * *

In answer to your letter, I have given birth to a baby weighing ten pounds. I hope this is satisfactory.

* * *

I cannot get sick pay, I have six kids, can you tell me why this is?

* * *

I am forwarding my marriage certificate and my two children, one of which is a mistake, as you will see.

* * *

I am pleased to say that my husband who was reported missing is now deceased.

* * *

This is my eighth child, and what are you going to do about it?

PENSIONS

I am writing these few lines for Mrs. J. who cannot write herself. She expects to be confined next week and can do with it.

*   *   *

Mrs. B. has no clothes and has not had any for a year. The clergy have been visiting her.

*   *   *

In reply to your letter, I have already cohabited with your officer, so far without result.

*   *   *

Please find out if my husband is dead, as the man I am now living with won't eat or do anything until he is certain.

*   *   *

Milk is wanted for my baby and his father cannot supply it.

*   *   *

Unless I get my husband's money I shall be forced to lead an immortal life."

*   *   *

I am sending my marriage certificate and six children. I had seven and one died which was baptised on a half sheet of notepaper.

SCHOOL

"Johnny," said the short-sighted teacher, "you can't help being poor, but I do wish you would ask your mother to patch your trousers with a cloth that would match."

"That b'aint no patch, miss," he replied. "That's me."

* * *

A very good little boy, fearing he would be late for school, said a little prayer. "Oh, Lord, don't let me be late for school. Oh, Lord, don't let me be late for school."

Then he stumbled and fell.

"Ode on," he said, "ay dey say shove."

* * *

The little girl was usually driven to school by her father, but as he was in bed with a cold, her mother drove her instead.

When they neared the school the child asked her mother where all the sods and bastards were that morning, as they didn't seem to have met any all the way.

* * *

The teacher was pointing out to the class that every boy who used his time profitably and cultivated a spirit of ambition had a chance of becoming Prime Minister.

"Joe," whispered one boy to another, "I'll sell yer my chance for a bob."

* * *

A parson visiting a school asked a class of young children: "How old am I?"

"Forty," said one boy, promptly.

"And what makes you so sure?"

"Well," said the boy, "I've got a bruther who was twenty last wik, an' 'e's a bit saft, an' you'm twice as saft as 'e is."

* * *

A superior lady visitor was asking questions at a church school.

"And what would you like to be when you grow up, little boy?"

"A sailor, lady."

"And why would you like to be a sailor?"

"So's I con' ave a wife in ev'ry port."

SCHOOL

It was scripture time. Asked to write down the events following the Last Supper, one boy wrote briefly: "Waeshin' up an' dryin'."

*   *   *

The schoolmaster had not decided in which class the new boy should be placed. "Sit there for the present," he said indicating an empty seat.

Came the afternoon session, the boy was still seated where he had been told. "Why didn't you go home to your dinner?" enquired the master.

"Oh," replied the boy, "I was waiting for the present."

*   *   *

The boys found a tramp asleep under the hedge alongside the school playing field.

"I wonder what 'ed say when he woke up," said one boy thoughtfully, "if somebody cut 'is yed off while 'e was aslape."

*   *   *

School inspector testing powers of observation: "Give me a number, boys. Any number."

Given the number 76, he transposed it on the blackboard to 67. No one appeared to notice the difference, so he tried again. Given 48, he wrote it down as 84. After several more numbers had been transposed with the same lack of comment he asked for just one more number.

"Thairty-three," shouted a boy at the back, "and muck that abaht if thee cost."

Please taycher, our 'ouse 'as bin cumdenumed, an' we lived up Aunt Fabe's back." (Aunt Phoebe's backyard.)

"I want you to write an essay on King Alfred," a teacher told a class of girls, "but I don't want anything about the cakes."

One bright girl's essay read: "King Alfred was a very great and good King. He did a great deal for England. One day he was out walking and got lost, but at last he came to a wood-cutter's cottage. The husband was out, but the woman was at home; but the least said about this the better."

79

SCHOOL

A tight-fisted farmer who was also a member of the Education Committee, visited the local school.

"What is nothing?" he asked a class of small boys.

"Please, sir," one youngster said promptly. "It's what yo' gid me when I 'eld yer 'oss for yer the other day."

*   *   *

Writing an essay on the Duke of Wellington, a schoolboy set down the information that the great soldier was given a splendid funeral; it took six men to carry the beer (bier).

*   *   *

The subject was mental arithmetic.

"If I had four apples in one hand and four in the other, how many should I have altogether?" asked the teacher.

"Two bloody 'ondfuls," came one answer.

*   *   *

A boy at Sunday School had been misbehaving.

"Remember," said the teacher, "you can't hide anything from God. He can see when you are naughty. In fact, God can see everything."

"Con He see down our cellar?" said the boy.

"Certainly He can."

"You'm a liar, then . . . 'cos we ay got one."

*   *   *

The teacher showed one of his pupils a picture of Niagara Falls. "Just think, boy," he said, "hundreds of millions of gallons of water goes over those Falls every day."

"Well, sir," said the boy, "lookin' at the picture, I cor see anythin' to stop 'em!"

*   *   *

"What's a miracle?" asked the lady visitor, examining a class of small children in the village school.

"Please, miss, I know," said a little girl. "Mother says as 'ow it ull be a miracle if yo' don't marry the new curate."

> *"Please, sir, we 'en flitted out o' that 'ouse we's livin'*
> *in now, an' gone into that 'un as 'as tumbled down."*

Asked what was meant by a census, a little boy explained: "It's a man a-goin' from dore to dore increasin' the population."

* * *

A schoolmistress told a mother that her little boy was often heard swearing.

"Well, I doe know wheer 'e 'ears it," said the mother. "Is feyther doe swear an' I doe swear, but if yo' 'ear 'im agen, send for me an' I'll gie the little bugger a bloody good 'idin'."

* * *

Schoolmaster: "Where do you live now, Jones?"

"Please, sir, the middlemust o' them fower 'ousen down our rode."

* * *

The schoolboy ran into the house:

"Eh, muvver . . . Our babby's bin an gone an' broke my spade."

" 'Ow did he do that?"

" 'E dey duck when I 'it 'im on the 'ead wi' it."

> *"I'm gettin' on wi' me sums at scule. I've got to the*
> *goosinters."*

Sunday school teacher: "Can any boy tell me what must precede baptism?"

"Please, sir . . . a babby."

* * *

"Please taycher, I think I sholl be leavin' soon."

"What makes you say that, Tommy?"

"Well, Miss, me mother's bernt the coal'ouse dore an' the cubberd dores, an' faether's a-choppin' down the stairs this mornin'. We allus leave after we've bernt the stairs."

SCHOOL

Little girl explaining her brother's absence from school: "It's 'is 'ead, teacher. Mother told me to tell yer as 'e's 'ad it on an' off ever since 'e was born."

*　　*　　*

The backward class in the old days really was backward. The teacher drew an 'O' on the board and asked a boy what figure it was:

"Tha's a bowl, Miss" (meaning hoop).

She put the figure one in front to make ten:

"Now what it it?"

"Tha's the stick what gos wi' the bowl to mek it goo."

*　　*　　*

"How many seasons in the year, Tommy?"

"Tew, sir–football and cricket."

SPORT

"W'at an they a-takin'?" shouted the new arrival to a fisherman who had been at the riverside for some time.

"They ay a-takin' ony notice, that's wot they'm a-takin'."

* * *

An old collier who had been a keen pigeon flyer all his life was on his deathbed. The vicar had arrived to give spiritual consolation.

"Sholl we 'ave wings, parson," enquired the collier, "in this 'ere next world yo' tork about?"

Assured that there was undoubted scriptural authority for the view that angels had wings, he said:

"Well, parson. If yo' 'as wings and I 'as wings wen yo' come up I'll fly yer for a quid."

* * *

Several men were on a pit mound preparing for a pigeon flying contest. As the first birds were about to be released one man said to another, who was to time the start: "Get yer watch out quick, Joe, five seconds aye many minutes agooin' . . ."

Said one of the competitors: "If my blighters doe cum back whum I'll shoot 'em."

* * *

Despite many lessons, a golfer was making so little progress that he was on the point of giving up. "Don't do that," advised a friend. "Do what I do. When you are about to drive off the tee, keep on saying to yourself over and over again, I shall drive this ball 150 yards, I shall drive this ball 150 yards. Then, when you've done that, take your iron and say, I will get on the green this shot. Repeat it again and again and you'll get there all right."

"Ah," said the despondent one, "it may be all right for you, but you don't know what a bloody liar I am."

* * *

A man fishing in the canal became irritated by the continued presence of a bystander.

"Yo've bin a-watchin' me all mornin'. If you'm that interested, why doe yo' tek up fishin' yerself?"

"Arr, I would," the other assured him. "Ony I ay got the patience."

83

SPORT

"Where are yer wheelin' the grandfather's clock to?" was the enquiry from an old man going towards the pit mounds for some pigeon racing that was in progress.

"Me waetch 'as stopped," was the answer, "an' I'm goin' to time the lad's wummers."

*　　*　　*

Two young men who were assisting at a village treat got some of the boys together for a game of football. Each young man chose a side and acted as captain. The sides were complete all except one, who had to be chosen out of the remaining two. "Doe 'ave 'im," said one of the two. "E's no good; he clanes 'is teeth."

*　　*　　*

"Bin yo' refereeing, or am I?" the referee at a football match demanded of a very excited spectator who kept criticising his decision.

"Neither on us," was the reply.

*　　*　　*

Bill and Joe were great pigeon flying rivals. One day Bill announced in the pub that he had just bought a new pigeon. "Whe'er am yo' keepin' it then?" Joe asked, a bit narked. "Yo'er loft's full up, ay it?"

"Arr," said Bill. "But I've got it in me bedroom, an' it ay ser bad, cos afore I goo ter werk of a mornin' I loose it fer a fly round the park."

Joe smiled knowingly: "Now I know you'm a liar. The park gates doe open till nine."

*　　*　　*

It was the morning after the first Zeppelin raid on the Black Country in the 1914-18 war.

"Did yer get the Zepps at Tip'on last night?"

"Oh, ah. They paed us a visit."

"Did they dew ony damage tew ony on yer?"

"Well they killed the ode 'ooman, but they dey touch the pigeons, so it might a bin wuss."

84

SPORT

"I'm drawn to play in the handicap with Colonel Black," the golfer informed his caddy. "What sort of a player is he?"

"Him?" scoffed the caddy. "The Colonel cor play for nuts. 'E's a rotten player."

"Well, that's all right then, I shall easily beat him."

"Yo' wo'," said the caddy.

"If I ay theer, yo' wait till I ay a-comin'."

Unable to beat the local squire at golf, the parson became very disheartened.

"Never mind," said the squire, who was a much older man, "you'll be called upon to bury me some day."

"Yes," said the parson, despondently: "and it will be your hole then!"

*　　*　　*

"Where's yer brother?" enquired a mother, from a boy who had just returned from skating.

"Well, mother," was the reply. "It's like this. If the ice is as thick as he thinks it is, he's skating. But if it's as thin as I think it is, he's swimming."

*　　*　　*

A Black Countryman and a Londoner were fishing close together.

Said the Londoner: "It's getting very dark, I think we shall have a storm."

"Doost?"

"No; rain, you fool!"

They adjourned to the nearby inn and ordered bread and cheese.

"I cort ate today," said the Black Countryman.

"You're a liar," snapped the Londoner. "You only caught one."

TRAVEL

Workman returning from work on a very crowded bus: "By gum, Joe, theer ay auf a crowd. 'Ere"s the conductor acummin' given' 'em tickets. I 'ope 'e's sode out afore 'e gets to we."

* * *

Travelling late on the local train, a woman remarked to a fellow passenger that the train was being driven very fast.

"Dun yo' reckon it's saef?"

"Oh, this ay fast," she was told. "It's our Bill a-drivin'. Yo' shud cum on 'is traen when 'e's 'ad a drop o' beer, then yo'd know about it."

* * *

"Conductor, ring the bell. You've taken me past," said an old lady who had given instructions where she wanted to stop.

"If yo'll stay a bit longer," she was told, "we'll tek yer future an' all, missis."

* * *

Two workmen returning home from work on the bus.

"Why, Bill, wotever's the matter wi' yo'. Yo' ay got any taeth."

"Yo' ony just noticed? I was in sich a 'urry to catch the bus this mornin' I forgot to put 'em in. Cor, I ay auf 'ungry. I'm a-bringin' me dinner 'ome for me tay."

* * *

A very tired man on his way home from work boarded a very crowded bus and hung on the strap, hoping shortly to get a seat. Stage after stage was passed and no one alighted. At last, in desperation, he glared at his fellow passengers and burst out: "Blast it . . . ay none on yer got any 'omes?"

* * *

A stranger, taking what he hoped was a short cut over some pit mounds, enquired from a boy the way to Tipton.

"Yo' get inter that 'ere rode as yo' con just see from 'ere, an yer cums across a sign post."

"That ay no good, I cor read."

"Oh, it doe matter; theer's nuthin' on it."

86

TRAVEL

Two ladies about to get on a bus kept motioning one another to get on first. The conductor lost patience. "Why the 'ell doe yer toss fer it? We'm got plenty o' time, we'm ony a quarter of an hour late."

*　　*　　*

A traveller had a grudge against the Railway Company.

"I've dun it acrost 'em this time," he exulted to a passenger. "I took a return ticket an' I ay agooin' back."

*　　*　　*

Sent by his boss to enquire the time of the next bus to Birmingham, the messenger returned all hot and bothered.

"Gaffer," he stammered, "if yo' maen to catch the next bus to Brummagem yo'll 'ave to move like the clappers, cos it's just gone."

*　　*　　*

Two Black Country mates who had had a big win in a Sweepstake, were celebrating with a holiday in the States. They had a room near the top of a skyscraper hotel and, this being during Prohibition, had hidden a bottle of whisky in their bedroom before going off to see the sights. When they got back they found that the lifts were out of order and, impatient to get at the whisky, decided to climb the stairs.

"Come on, Joe, if ween got to do it, let's get at it like a pig at a tater," said one, and off they went. After negotiating several flights, they had to stop for a rest.

"We cor go on like this, let's tell a tael on every landin' to give our legs a chance."

At every landing a tale was told, and they arrived at length on the last floor but one to their room.

"Well, Joe, we've tode a lot of rotten taels, but I've got a good 'un at last."

"Let's 'ave it, " said Joe.

"We'm forgot the bloody kay!"

TRAVEL

Two Gornal men on a tandem bicycle.

"Bill," said the one riding on the front saddle, "it's damned 'ard peddlin' up this 'ill."

"Ar, it's a steep 'ill orlright," said Bill from the back. "I've put the braek on so we shor goo backwards."

*　　*　　*

A man who hadn't been on a train before joined the queue at the booking office. A woman in front of him asked for "Sally Oak, single." Following her example, he said to the booking clerk: "Ali Bradley, married."

The clerk naturally asked him where he wanted to go. "W'at the 'ell 'as that got to do wi' yo'?" he said. "Yo' dey ask 'er."

*　　*　　*

Having reluctantly agreed to drive a drunk home on a foggy night, a hire-car driver discovered that the fog was thicker than he thought, so he decided to fetch his brother to walk in front of the car. "Yo' doe want to bother 'im on a night like this," said the drunk. "I'll do it meself."

*　　*　　*

A man was getting off a bus and before he had released his hold of the rail the bus started and he continued to cling to it.

Came the voice of a friend from within the bus: "What am yer tryin' ter dew, Joe? Yo' doe waent to tek the bus with yer, dun yer?"

*　　*　　*

A coach was loading a party of Black Country holiday-makers at Weston-super-Mare.

"Where am yo' teking that lot?" a Gornal man asked the driver.

"To Burnham," he was told.

"Well, 'ode on a minit an' yo' con tek my missis."

"We dey 'arf goo acomin' back in that theer chara."

88

"Yo'er fiddlin' and fussin' about 'as maed us lose the train, an' there's a 'our to waet for the next," complained a man to his wife.

"That's your fault," she told him. "If yer 'adn't rushed me we shouldn't 'ave 'ad to waert so long for the next train."

* * *

The bus driver over-ran a recognised stopping place, where several people were waiting. The conductor slid back the glass panel and said to the driver: "Ay, mate, in case yo' ay noticed, there's a stoppin' place back theer."

* * *

Some twenty people were waiting in the queue when the bus pulled up, but nobody offered to go upstairs. Said the conductor: "I shud think yo' lot all live in bungalows."

* * *

A Tipton boy who had never been on any boat but a canal boat, was taken on a steamer during a seaside holiday. Eyeing the craft from the landing stage, he turned to his father and said: "Faether, where's the 'oss?"

* * *

A number of chainmakers were travelling home from work on the bus.

"I think the sates on this bus are the comfortablist I ever sot on," said one.

"Yo' doe say that when you'm agoin' to waerk Yo' say they'm as 'ard as ode 'ell."

"Well, that's different, ay it?"

* * *

Conductor to old lady boarding a double-decker bus: "Doe 'urry, mother, but maek haeste, an' if yo' ay careful 'ow you'm getting up them steps, yo'll be at the bottom as soon as yo' gets to the top."

* * *

It was the custom for half a dozen workmen who were pals to travel in the same railway carriage from Wednesbury station to Dudley.

On one occasion, as the train approached Dudley Port, one of the workmen announced the loss of his ticket. A fellow workman, signifying to the others that he had picked it up, said gravely: "What am yer goin' ter do, Joe? We shon soon 'ave the ticket collector 'ere."

TRAVEL

After various suggestions, it was decided that the ticketless man should hide under the seat, which he did. The collector at Dudley Port, duly handed six tickets, commented that there were only five passengers.

"Oh, that's all right," said the chief leg-puller. "The other chap's under the sate; he likes that way better than sitting down on it like we."

* * *

Bus conductor to driver: "Cum on, Bill, let's get away. There's somebody behind wants to catch the bus."

* * *

Two women relating how they had spent the Bank Holiday:

Said one: "Me an' my mon dey dew nothin' till six o'clock, an' then we went to the Blue Pig an' got a few drinks inside we, an' cum wum an' went to bed."

"Oh," said the other. "We 'ad a grand time at the raeces. I forget the name o' the plaece, but we went to it by train. It wore about twenty miles away on a single line, an' we dey meet another traen all the way."

* * *

"How far to the station, boy?"

"Ten minutes' good walk if yo' run."

* * *

A lady, being driven by a temporary chauffeur, enquired his name. "Clarence," he told her.

"I never call chauffeurs by their Christian name," the lady said emphatically. "What's your surname?"

"Darling."

"Drive on, Clarence!" she said.

* * *

A small man in a crowded bus sat next to a very fat lady.

"If yo' was a real gen'leman," remarked the fat lady, "yo'd get up and mek room for a 'ooman to sit down."

"If yo' was a lady," was the reply, "yo'd get up an' mek room for three."

90

TRAVEL

A motorist came to a flooded dip in the road and asked an urchin if it was deep.

"No, it aye dip," said the boy. But before the car was halfway across the water was up to the doors. "I thought you said it wasn't deep," the driver shouted angrily to the boy.

"It aye dip, I tell yer. Ow'er duck was on it a bit agoo an' it ony cum up to 'is middle."

"The bus as I cum ter werk on this mornin' dae tern up."

"And where do you think you are going?' a policeman enquired of a motorist he had stopped going the wrong way in a one way street.

"I doe rightly know," said the motorist. "But I must be laet . . . t'others am all comin' back."

*　　*　　*

Arriving at a junction of three roads and not knowing which to take, a motorist waylaid a collier returning from the pit.

"Where should I get to if I took the road to the left?" he enquired.

"I doe know," was the reply.

"Well, suppose I decide to turn to the right, where would that take me?"

"I caw tell you that," said the collier.

Exasperated, the motorist asked where he would get to if he drove straight ahead. The collier still had no information, and that made his questioner really angry. "My good man," he snapped, "you don't appear to know anything."

"Well, perhaps I doe," said the man. "But I ay lost like yo'."

*　　*　　*

After sitting in a stationary bus for half an hour, a passenger sought out the conductor.

"What time did yo' say this bus starts?"

"One forty-five."

"Ar! But dun yo' mean today or tomorrer?"

TRAVEL

A motorist enquiring his way to a certain town was told by the man from whom he made the enquiry that he didn't know whether the road he was on led there or not. Deciding to take a chance the motorist drove on. He was just getting into top when he heard a loud shout calling him back. Reversing a good fifty yards, he found that the man had been joined by another.

"This is my pal," was the greeting. "I've asked 'im for yer . . . and 'e doe know neyther."

*   *   *

Bus conductor at terminus: "Ere yer are for weer you'm gooin'; all in 'ere for 'ere, get out."

*   *   *

Overheard at the bus terminus: "Am yer gooin' or cummen back, or stoppin' 'ere? If you'm stoppin' 'ere yo'd better cum with me."

*   *   *

A traveller who rushed onto the station too late to get into the train, chased after it down the line. A quarter of an hour later, when he returned, a porter grinned at him.

"Well," he said, "yo' dey ketch it?"

"No," said the man, "But I dey auf mek the blighter puff."

*   *   *

Woman at Moxley telling stranger the best way to get to Bilston: "Bilston, let's see. Bin as yo' bin as yo' bin, yo'd better goo right on."

*   *   *

When aircraft were a novelty:

"Ay, ow'er kid, yo' look at them plaenes. They ay auf flyin' a depth."

*   *   *

A mother was helping down child after child from the top deck of a bus. Said the conductor:

"Ay, missis, 'an yo' got a nest up theer?"

92

TRAVEL

A lady, explaining that her two sons had sailed for the States, said that they had gone sewerage (meaning steerage).

"Never mind," said one of her listeners, "they'll soon get manured to it."

* * *

"That's the nighest way," a loafer on a cross roads told a motorist enquiring the way to Tipton. "But if yo' want the best road yo' should tek this other 'un. But there again, if I was agoin' to Tipton, I shouldn't a started from 'ere at all."

* * *

Two factory workers on a trip to Blackpool decided to have a bathe. "My God, Joe!" said one to the other, as they entered the water. "Yo' ay auf grimy. Yo' con do with a waesh."

"Ah," said Joe. "But doe yo' forget, I'm three 'ear oder than yo'."

* * *

Motorist to bus driver: "Dun yo' want all the blinkin' road?"
Bus driver: "Yes, mate, when yo've dun with it."

"I'm glad I cum now, else I shouldn't be 'ere."

"Dun ye 'ave auf fare for children?"
"Yes, under fourteen."
"Oh, tha's orlright, I's only got five."

* * *

Told by the conductor, no smoking in the lower deck, the passenger said: "Cor yer see as I bay smokin'?"

"Well yo've got a pipe in yo're mouth."

"I got shoes on me feet, ay I? But I bay walkin'."

93

TRAVEL

A motorist ignored a traffic signal and when stopped by a policeman said he never took any notice of them, anyway.

"Oh, you don't" said the officer. "Let's have a look at your driving licence."

"I've bin drivin' for fifteen years an' I ay bothered ter get one."

"That's a very serious offence, sir. You'd better show me your insurance certificate."

"I doe 'ave no insurance. Doe believe in it," said the motorist.

At this point the man's wife piped up from the back: "Yo' doe waent tew tek ony notice of 'im, officer–'e allus talks like that when 'e's drunk."

WORK

The store manager glared wrathfully at the young assistant:
"I distinctly told you you could take seven clear days holiday. What's the idea of being away for ten?"

"It's all right, sir. Three of 'em wus foggy."

* * *

A workman who worked for a small employer said he worked eight hours a day and didn't mind a bit.

"P'raps in time you'll become a gaffer like me," the employer told him. "Then 'ave to work 12 hours, an' 'ave the worry as well as the work."

"If I got yer a job an' sent yer to it, yer 'ouldn't goo."

An employer tried to turn an excellent workman from bouts of drinking, lecturing him severely and at great length. When he had finished, the erring workman remarked: "Well, gaffer, yo've sed a lot about beer, but what I waents to tell yo' is that with all yer tork yo' aye convinced me as I doe like it."

* * *

A working man who had set up in business on his own became very prosperous, moved to a better district and bought a pretentious motor car. Anxious to show off the car, and his wife's costly furs into the bargain, they drove round the squalid streets of their former neighbourhood. Unfortunately, the car 'conked' and he had to get out and turn the starting handle. A one-time neighbour chanced to look out of her bedroom window. Seeing the show-off twirling the handle and his wife sat upright in her furs, she shouted: "Ay, we doe want no moosic in this street. Clear off and tek yer monkey with yer."

* * *

"Can you use a shovel?" an employer enquired of an applicant for a job.

"Oh, ah," he was assured. 'I doe know anythin' better to fry a bit o' baecon on, when yo' ay got nara fryin' pon."

95

WORK

A workman who had overslept, dressed hurriedly and, anxious not to lose a 'quarter,' rushed out into the darkness, promptly falling over on the frosty pavement. As he rose to his feet, a passer-by enquired if he was hurt. He said he thought he was only shook up a bit. Then, looking down at his trousers which, in his haste he had put on behind before, he added: "No, I doe think I'm 'urt very bad, but I must 'ave gid meself a devil of a twist."

* * *

Electric welding had just come into chain making. "Well," said one chainmaker, scornful of the new method, "they con say w'at they liken, but there's a good mony as 'ould rather 'ave the damned links 'ommered than frizzled."

* * *

A somewhat impulsive master builder noticed a man on the site apparently idling away his time at a brazier. "We don't want any idlers on this job," he said. "Here's your day's money. Now clear off."

A little later on, the site foreman sought him out. "Yo' know that mon yo' gid a day's waeges too, gaffer . . ." he began.

The builder stopped him abruptly. "It's no use you pleading on his behalf. I don't care if he happens to be a relation of yours, I'm not having loungers like that working for me."

"That's just it," said the foreman. "He wor waerkin' for yo'. 'E was just a bloke loafin' about lookin' for waerk and 'opin' he wouldn't find it. If'n 'e meets many more like yo', 'e woe naed to nither."

* * *

A foundry worker, eating his dinner in the canteen, noticed a mate limping badly.

"What an' yo' bin an' dun?"

"I ay dun nuthin'. I've got a nail in me shoe."

"Well, why doe yo' knock it down?"

"What . . . in me dinner 'our? Think I'm saft?"

* * *

Gossiping on the pit bank at breakfast time, one of a group of colliers felt that he was being left out of the conversation.

WORK

"Somebody in the night stole a cockerel and four hens out o' our fowl pen," he announced. "Me missis waeks up an' 'er says to me, 'them fowl am quiet this mornin', I cor 'ear a sound. It's just a-gettin' light, an' the cockerel ay crowin', I wonder what's up.' Anyrode, when I got up I went to look an' there they was–all gone."

"Did yer go across the road an' tell the ode sargeant afore yo' cum to waerk this mornin'?"

"No, 'e dey live 'ere then, it's 34 'ear ago."

*　　*　　*

"Let's 'ave a swig out o' yoer can, Bill," said a workman to his mate.

" 'Ere y'are, Joe; the whisky's at the bottom."

"I'm glad yo' tode me. I'll drink from the bottom fust, then."

*　　*　　*

"An' yo' got a job yet?"

"O, ah, I've got a good 'un at last, as a corsetiere."

"A corsetiere? That's a woman's job."

"I've got it, any rode."

"Wot dun yer 'ave ter dew?"

"O, I ony as ter stond by the reserved sates at the pictures an' wen anybody tak's a sate an' 'e ay got a ticket, I just ses yo' cor sit 'ere."

*　　*　　*

"If you'm a waent'n a job," said a man to a work-shy neighbour, "I knows wheer there's one gooin' fer a right 'ond mon."

"Tay no good tellin' me," said the other hastily. "I'm left 'onded."

*　　*　　*

A dim-witted messenger was sent by a carpenter to buy a brace and bit. When he got to the ironmonger's, he transposed the requirement into a brazen bitch. The ironmonger sent back a message that the brazen bitches were all sold out, but he had a good line in fast cats.

WORK

During the first World War, the following letter was sent by a Black Country firm to the Ministry of Munitions:

"During this great war we have done many things that aforetime we had considered almost impossible. We have turned ploughshares into swords, made night into day, made bricks without straw, turned water into wine, and ale into compound for the refreshing of labour.

"We have resurrected machine tools and taught them to rise and sing; we have imported proud Americans, we have salvaged destitute Belgians.

"We have gathered in and utilised barbers, circus proprietors, aboriginals from the Antipodes, and some of the 'Best People'.

"We have made women into mechanics, and mechanics into supermen such as may be found at the Ministry of Munitions. We have diluted our labour, both male and female, until we have workers of the combined sex and of neither sex.

"We have honoured the King and strafed his enemies, but we stand today hopelessly cast down by your suggestion that we should cut 2-inch Module pitch Aeroplane Engine gear with a $2\frac{1}{2}$ Module Cutter.

"Yours in chastened spirit,

ICHABOD."

(From a 1919 Journal)

WORK

A navvy with an unusually large nose was working on some excavations.

"There's a fly on yer nose," said his mate.

"Well, knock it off, then. You'm nearer to it than I am."

* * *

A workman being lowered down a well on a rope yelled that he wanted to come up again.

"What for?" said the man holding the rope.

"Never yo' mind. If yo' doe stop lettin' me down when I tell yer, I'll cut the bloody rope."

* * *

Times were hard, and a group of unemployed were standing at the gates of a factory, hoping to be taken on. "Sorry chaps," the manager told them. "The fact is, I can hardly find enough work for the men I already have." As he turned back into the works, one little man ran after him: "Well, gaffer, I reckon yo' can find me a job wi'out ony trouble, cos the bit I sholl dew woe mek ony difference."

* * *

A foreman on a building site thought he would do a good turn to an out of work mate. "There's no real vacancy," he said. "But come tomorrow at starting time and mess about, and I'll put you on the daily pay sheet." His mate did as he was told and the following evening the foreman asked him how he had got on.

"Oh, all right," he said. "But tomorrer yo' must gie me a shovel to lean on like what the rest 'ave got."

* * *

A toolmaker was instructed to try his hand at making a very difficult tool. In due course the man returned to the office and said: "Gaffer, I've done me best, but there ay any mon livin' as con mak a tool like that. Yo'll 'ave to buy one after all."

99

WORK

A gang of men were working on a sewerage scheme. After the mid-day meal one of them lay down for a siesta, using a drain pipe as a pillow.

"My gum, this 'ere drainpipe ay auf 'ard. It doe rest yer much."

"Well, yer fule," said his mate, "it serves yer right. Yo' should stuff some straw in it, like I do."

*   *   *

An unemployed collier was assisting in the removal of some furniture from one house to another. The distance being short did not warrant the engagement of the usual 'remover'. A handcart was requisitioned for the purpose of transferring the piano.

"Where bin yer gooin' with that pianner, Joe?" said a friend to the pusher of the handcart.

"Cor yer see, yer fule? I'm gooin' to 'ave me moosic lesson."

*   *   *

Workman arriving at a mate's house to break the news of an accident: "Joe aye in, is 'e?"

"No, 'e aye," snapped the lady of the house. " 'e's at work, wheer yo' ought to be."

"Well, he soon will be in," said the caller. " 'E's just 'ad 'is leg broke, an' they'm a-bringin' 'im wum on a stretcher."

*   *   *

Instead of pulling a drowning man out of the canal, a man on the towpath rushed off to the works where the drowning man was employed.

"Yore man, Joe Smith, 'as bin drowned," he told the foreman. "Can I 'ave 'is job?"

"Yo'm too late," said the foreman. "The chap as pushed 'im in 'as got it."

100

WORK

A man who got a job at the gas works was given a master key and told to go round the district and empty the slot meters. Nothing was heard of him for a fortnight, and when he eventually showed up the cashier wanted to know why he hadn't at least been in for his wages.

"Oh," said the man. "I dey know as I 'ad waeges as well. I only come back for another kay, as I'n lost the one yo' gid me at fust."

*   *   *

A father and son were employed at the same works, and usually came to work together. One morning the son arrived by himself, and was asked by the manager where his father was:

"O, I doe think he'll be 'ere this mornin'."

"Perhaps he will come after breakfast," said the manager hopefully.

The son shook his head, "It's like this 'ere. Las' night I forgot to chop the wood for the fire, and this morning faether was a bit angry and said he'd do it 'imself. Some on it was a bit 'ard to break an' he put one long piece across the top o' the well an' jumped on it an' it broke an' . . . well, I doe reckon he'll cum to work this mornin'."

*   *   *

A skilled workman who knew his own worth, was in trouble for gambling.

"Joe," said the works manager, "unless you give up this persistent gambling, I shall have to sack you." "I'll bet yo' a quid yo' don't," was the challenging reply.

"I sholl 'ave bin 'ere a fortnit cum termorrer, an' ay felt well one day since."

A puddler knocked off work because of heat. When he got home he quarrelled with his wife because she had let the fire out.

WORK

Colliers going off their shift at the coalface with a long jaunt in front of them to the shaft, discovered some tools badly in need of re-sharpening. Unwilling to be bothered with carrying them, they chalked up a notice for the men on the next shift.

"Overlooked these tools when we was comin' off. Bring em along when yo' come."

Next day they found their message replaced by another: "We dey see these tools when we knocked off so we've lef' 'em for yo' after all."

*　　*　　*

Two workmen who worked at separate tube works were arguing as to which works produced the most wonderful tubes. Said one: "The toobs we mek at our works bin so big as the 'ole in the middle weighs two tun."

"That's nothin'," said the other, "we meks 'em so small as yo' cor see the 'ole in the middle. Why, we 'as to work to thousandths of a inch."

"How many thousandths be there in a inch, then?"

"I doe rightly know, but there must be millions."

*　　*　　*

Working in a foundry yard, a spark from the cupola dropped on the cloth cap of one of the workmen. Before he was aware of it the cap began to smoulder.

"Sammy's cap's afire," yelled a workman.

"Doe bother," said another, "the waeter in his yed ull soon put it out."

*　　*　　*

A collier on his way to work met a fellow workman walking towards him.

"Where are yer gooin' this mornin', Bill?"

"Goin' to work, yer fule. Where dun yo' think I'm goin'?"

"But yo'm gooin' the wrong rode; yo'm on the way wum."

"Oh, arr, so I am. I turned me back to the wind to lite me pipe an' I forgot to turn round again."

WORK

Two bricklayers repairing a well, decided it was not worth while to put down a scaffolding. They thought that if one of them held the other by the feet the repair, being near the top of the well, could be satisfactorily completed.

One held the feet of his mate and the other started on the job. The man at the top, feeling his grip slipping, shouted: "Oud on a bit, Joe, while I spit on me 'onds."

*　*　*

A manufacturer placed his son in the care of an experienced workman to learn the business. After a few weeks he asked the man how his son was progressing. "No 'ow," said the man. "I've tode him all I know, an' now 'e knows nothin'."

*　*　*

A man whose usual occupation was that of steering a boat on the canal was pulling his big barge along the tow-path. He was accosted by a friend from the canal bridge. "Ain't yer workin' today, Bill?" "No," said Bill, "the old 'oss is bad, so I ay workin' today."

*　*　*

Said the foreman of one works to the foreman of another: "Our gaffer's bin kickin' up a rumpus about so many men comin' in to their work after the 'bull's' finished blowin'. But I put it right–I've arranged as the last man in sholl blow the damn thing."

*　*　*

Shop manager to new assistant: "What's the matter with you? Every time you see a 6 you call it a 2. You near-sighted or something?"

"No, it ay that, gaffer. It's 'abit. Y'see I used ter werk in a ladies' shoe shop?"

*　*　*

During the depression of the 'thirties, a Yank in Bilston was asked by a local where he came from:

"The State of Ohio. What place is this?"

"Bilston."

"Well, friend . . . what State is that in?"

"A bloody awful state–we'm all out of work."

103

WORK

The factory hand had volunteered to learn first aid.

"If there was an explosion in the boiler house and a man was blown into the air, what would you do?" he was asked.

"I'd wait fer 'im to cum down," was the prompt reply.

*   *   *

A clerk who was off sick was visited at home by a colleague: "Now just yo' git well an' doe worry yer 'ead about things at the office," he was told. "We'm all gooin' ter muck in an' tek care o' yo're werk . . . soon as we con find out what it is yo' dun."

*   *   *

"So you want a job as night watchman? What makes you think you would be suitable?"

"Well, for one thing, Master, the least noise wakes me up."

*   *   *

After being on the dole for a long time, Jack finally got a job as a 'bus conductor. His first day's takings were only a few pence, and he was asked for an explanation.

"When I was out o' work," he said indignantly, "nobody 'ud spake tew me. Now I've got this job they'm a-wavin' tew me at every stop. I ay tekin' no notice. Let 'em walk, like what I 'ad tew when I was out o' werk."

*   *   *

An out of work bricklayer was given a job of building a wall 6ft. high and strong enough to stand a high wind. When the work was finished and the customer came along to inspect, he had every right to be astonished.

"I asked you to build a 6ft. wall," he gasped, "but I never expected it to be 6ft. high and 6ft. wide. What's the idea?"

"Well, gaffer," he was told, "yo' said yo' wanted it ter stand a 'igh wind, an' the way it is now, if it blows over it'll still be stondin' up."

WORK

"I see as Jack's gorra new Cortina G.T."

"Oh arr; werz 'e werk?"

" 'E doe work, 'e's gorra bisness."

* * *

Two roadsweepers were hard at work when one of them found a pound note in the gutter.

" 'Arvers," shouted his mate, before he could hide it.

"All rite," said the finder. "Yo' sholl 'ave the next."

* * *

During the war when it was compulsory to fit blackouts to the windows, a workman awoke, forgot the circumstances, and went off to sleep again until daylight. When he finally roused himself and went downstairs, it was daylight and nine o'clock. He hurried to work and apologised to the foreman for losing a 'quarter'. "That's all right," said the foreman. "But weer won yer all yesterday?"

* * *

Two men at a brewery loading the same cart with grain, were using wooden shovels supposed to hold a bushel. The customer whose cart was being loaded questioned whether one of the shovels held that quantity. "Oh, we'll soon put that right," said one loader to another. "Change shovels, Bill."

The customer was satisfied.

* * *

Getting up early to go to work, a miner shouted to his wife: "Missus, I cor get this 'ere new bottle as yo've bought for me tay into me pocket."

"Well, pore a drap out then, yer fule."

* * *

" 'Ere yo'," said an angry workman to his mate. "Did yo goo an' tell the manager I was a bloody liar?"

"No, I dey. I thought 'e bloody well knew."

WORK

A man taking a few days holiday, strolled past the building site where his pal was employed. Catching sight of him, he said: "Bost me, 'Erbert. I dey think yo' werked that 'ard." "Ah," chuckled Herbert. "I con see I'se fooled yo' the same as 'Ise fooled the foreman. I'se carried this saeme 'odfull o' bricks up an' down the ladder all day, an' 'e thinks I'm werkin' ".

*　　*　　*

"I wish you'd come to the office in clothes that are a bit decent and tidy," the cashier told the clerk. "One of these days somebody will be taking you for the boss."

*　　*　　*

An applicant for a job in a pit was asked if he had worked in a pit before. "O, ah, I worked at the Jubilee," he replied.

He was then asked casually if the Jubilee were using the electric safety lamp.

"Doe ask me that," he said, "I worked on the day shift."

*　　*　　*

"We mek things at our plaece that goo all round the globe."

"What bin they then?"

"Lampshaedes."

*　　*　　*

" 'E's alus a-grumblin'," said one workman to another indicating the shop foreman.

"Well, why doe yer cuss 'im, loike I doo," said his mate.

The pair met later in the dinner-hour.

"I did what yo' said. I gid the foreman a damn good cussin'."

"Did it mak any difference?"

"Ar, it did. I got a wik's notice. If yo'n cussed 'im 'ow is it yo' dey get the sack?"

"Yo waernt such a fule as to cuss 'im so's 'e cud 'ear, wun yer? Yo' shouldn't a-done that. I ony cussed 'im w'en 'e wor theer."

WORK

The colliers were coming off the shift when Sammy, physically fit but mentally less alert than his comrades, was seen looking round in all sorts of odd corners as if he had lost something. When he was asked what was missing he answered that he had lost his wescut. After a thorough search had been made one of the colliers noticed that Sammy was still wearing the garment.

"Why, Sammy," he said, "yo've got yer wescut on."

"Well I'm dommed, so I 'ave," said Sammy. "If yo' hadn't tode me I should a gone wum without it."

15 QUICK LAUGHS

Artist Paul was in The Miners' Arms when he noticed what a fine head Aynuk had and decided that he'd like to paint him. On hearing Paul's request Aynuk was non-committal. Ayli encouraged his mate. "Goo on Aynuk, he wants ter paint yer Yed an' shoulders, yoe knowen, be a model. Ask 'im fer a couple o'quid. Yowed be famous".

Paul: Yes, I'll pay you a couple of pounds.

Ayli: Goo on our kid. It'll be th' easiest couple o' quid yow'll ever get.

Aynuk: Ar, it sounds all right but shall ah be able ter get the paint off me yed?

*   *   *

Aynuk and Ayli went with Age Concern on a holiday to Coblenz, Germany. Accommodation had been arranged with German families and on alighting from their coach on arrival Aynuk said:

"Well, I 'ope me 'ost con spake English".

Ayli: Ah, I 'ope 'er con cuss yoe cor.

*   *   *

Brierley Hill Alliance were engaged in a very hard match with Lye Town when one of the latter went off in the second half limping. Immediately the Alliance captain sent off one of his team.

"That's very sporting of you", remarked a supporter. "I expect you think that it will be better to beat them on equal terms".

"No, it ay that", replied the captain, "our blokes 'ave left their money in the changing room".

*   *   *

In the days before the widespread use of telephones local lay preacher Job Bloomer received a telegram one Saturday afternoon requesting him to fill in for a sick minister the following day. A pre-paid form for 15 words was enclosed. Job's first attempt with the address and confirmation "Yes" only came to 13 words, so, not wanting to waste two words he amended the message to "Yes, all right".

*   *   *

Teacher: Young Aynuk you have had a whacking every day so far this week. What have you got to say for yourself?

Young Aynuk: Ah ay arf glad its Friday.

Ayli encouraged Aynuk to enter his monster red currents in the local horticulture show. Aynuk was most disappointed to find that they had only been judged third in that section. He then found out that they had been mistakenly entered in the Tomato class.

*   *   *

Aynuk's wife's mother lived with them and had been off-colour for over a year during which time she complained every time her doctor visited her about her constantly aching joints and feelings on nausea: "Yoe doe do me no good at all".

In desperation the doctor brought in a geriatrics specialist who was accompanied by an attractive bright young nurse.

For a quarter of an hour the three professionals engaged the old lady in conversation which at first evoked no response but gradually an occasional grunt. Seeing this as a sign of having gained her confidence the doctor nodded to the specialist and left the room for the latter to conduct the examination.

Consultant: Come on now darling, take your clothes off. (There was no reply).

Consultant: Come on dear, off with your knickers. (Again, no response).

Consultant: Now Mrs. Cartwright, can't you hear what I'm saying?

Aynuk's mother in law: Oh ahr, ah con 'ear yer all right, ah thought yoe was spakin' ter that yung nuss.

*   *   *

Ayli: About this acorn.

Aynuk: Ahr, warra bout it?

Ayli: Weir dun yoe think ah shud plant it ter gie the moost shaird?

*   *   *

Blackpool landlady: As a whole this room is quite good don't you think?

Ayli: Ar missus, but as a bedroom it ay.

Ayli was studying the ravages of a violent thunderstorm on his allotment when his mate arrived to cheer him up.

Aynuk: Joby's patch is just as bad as yowern.

Ayli: How about Ezra's?

Aynuk: 'Isn is wuss. 'Is greenhouse has been shattered.

Ayli: It ay as bad as ah thought.

*   *   *

"Dearest Lizzie", wrote Aynuk, "I'd swim the cut for one look into your deep blue eyes. I'd walk through th'Earl's furnace for one touch of your tiny hand. I'd jump a crowners end for one word from your lovely lips.

Lots of love,
Aynuk.

P.S. I'll be over on Sunday night if it doesn't rain.

*   *   *

Aynuk: That better ma wench. Ah doe like ter see yower fairce all framed up.

Does it mean yoan forgid me fer cummin wum drunk?

Wife: Yoe keep yer distance. Ah'm oney smilin' ter gie me fairce a rest.

*   *   *

Young Aynuk: Ah ay gooen.

Teacher: Listen, I am not going, you are not going, they are not going. Do you understand?

Young Aynuk: Arh, there ay nobody gooen.

*   *   *

Aynuk: Yoan gorra loud overcoat on ay yer?

Ayli: Ah, ah'm goona buy a muffler ter goo wi' it.